Investigative Discourse Analysis

Investigative Discourse Analysis

Statements, Letters, and Transcripts

SECOND EDITION

Don Rabon

Tanya Chapman

Carolina Academic Press

Durham, North Carolina

Library of Congress Cataloging-in-Publication Data

Rabon, Don.
Investigative discourse analysis : statements, letters, and transcripts / Don Rabon and Tanya Chapman. -- 2nd ed.
p. cm.
Includes bibliographical references.
ISBN 978-1-59460-912-1 (alk. paper)
1. Discourse analysis. I. Chapman, Tanya. II. Title.
P302.R33 2012
401'.41--dc23 2011046986

Carolina Academic Press
700 Kent Street
Durham, NC 27701
Telephone (919)489-7486
Fax (919) 493-5668
www.cap-press.com

Printed in the United States of America
2021 Printing

Contents

Preface

In the ensuing years since the first edition of *Investigative Discourse Analysis,* a goodly number of requests for analyses have come our way. These analysis requests provide a vehicle to keep us in a hands-on mode, with each analysis serving as a learning experience. Additionally, we have been privileged to conduct investigative discourse analysis classes via traditional and distance learning formats on a continual basis to participants from a wide variety of backgrounds and topic area applications. Each offering has deepened our knowledge base and broadened the horizon for the use of investigative discourse analysis.

As a result, we have gained a proportional degree of productive lessons learned and enhanced applications. Our intent in this edition is to apply what we, and others involved in the analysis process, have gleaned through our endeavors and to present those dynamics in a format that will serve as a Rosetta Stone. Our goal is for this edition to be a continual resource, pairing terms, concepts, and definitions with actual narratives, transcripts, and letters. Consequently, when conducting an analysis in the realm of your responsibilities, you will be able to work from **example** to **term** to **definition,** or any combination thereof.

Consequently, we recommend you place your answer in the spaces that have been provided, make notes and references throughout as you process this text. The use of different-colored highlighters to identify various linguistic components is recommended. If we address a linguistic component that will have particular functionality for you, make a note of it in the margin right then and there. Don't lose the thought. If, as we address a new concept it crosses your mind that you perhaps saw that dynamic in a narrative, letter, or transcript in a previous chapter, stop and go back to look for it. In doing so you are taking the learning effectiveness of this text to the level where it will work most effectively for you.

As a result of what we have gleaned from conducting analyses and courses, we have endeavored to make this edition more personal and more challenging than the first. And if you are going make the effort to work your way through this process with us, you deserve to know why.

First, a most critical element of investigative discourse analysis is the mindset of the person conducting the analysis and subsequent interview. This realization is reflected strongly in the flow of this edition. Toward that end of obtaining the analyst's mindset, throughout the text you will find some tasks for you to complete. These tasks are designed to provide ancillary—though no less important—points for enhancing the analysis process. To accomplish this goal of conducting a productive analysis we have endeavored not to write in an impersonal style. As much as possible, via the written word, we want to be there with you as you progress through the material, the practical exercises, and examinations. To paraphrase Charles Dickens, we want it to seem as if we are there at your side right now each step of the way.

In reading the narratives, transcripts, letters, etc., you will find misspelling, typographical errors, and incorrect punctuation. Documents for analysis will not always come across your desk in the most pristine and grammatically correct condition. In our effort to present the text in a reality-based format, the documents are presented in their original condition, grammatical errors and all.

In that vein, as you progress you will discover we pose a large number of questions for which we do not provide the answers. In our classroom settings we do the same thing. The questions are designed to guide the participant not to look for *the* answer but rather *an* answer. Once we believe we have *the* answer, we cease thinking. Only when we recognize we have *an* answer do we continue to think and process. Investigative discourse analysis is all about thinking—asking what is there and what is not there.

Second, we have made the tasks, examinations, and the search for related elements more challenging as the text progresses. The intent in the first edition was to make it easier to reference an element and to find it within the document. We now know that the learning is in the struggle. To make it easier to find the components does not enhance the learning process. More to the matter, in the real world, statements, narratives, transcripts, and letters do not arrive for analysis with convenient reference markings within the body. Consequently, this delivery format allows for more realistic application. Think of this as *tough love.* In the end you will have a fuller understanding and a higher degree of proficiency. Hold that thought as we go forward.

Within the text there are ten chapters. Each chapter is formulated to take our study deeper into the analysis process. As our knowledge and application abilities grow, each chapter serves as a stepping stone to the next. It has been said time is what prevents everything from happening at once (Wheeler). Similarly in our journey through this text, everything cannot be *presented* at once. We have placed additional information at the locations best suited for assimilation and application. As an example, we will address pronouns, in part, in one chapter and have additional information regarding pronouns in subsequent chapters. Rest assured there is a method behind the madness.

The chapters are as follows:

Chapter 1: Terms, Concepts, and Definitions
A working knowledge of the related linguistic analysis terms is a significant step toward mastery of the analysis process.

Chapter 2: Obtaining the Individual's Narrative
Securing the narrative in the proper manner provides for a productive analysis and subsequent amplification.

Chapter 3: Analysis of Narrative by Its Form
In the analysis of a narrative, form really does follow function.

Chapter 4: Semantic Analysis of the Narrative
Every word is important. Every word has meaning.

Chapter 5: The Parts of Speech and the Analysis Process
The various parts of speech open doors and windows into the world of the teller of the tale.

Chapter 6: Amplification of the Narrative
Allowing the interviewee to *meet* his or her own words is the gold standard of the interview process.

Chapter 7: The Analysis Process and Alternate Forms of Documentation: Letters and Emails
Expanding the analysis process beyond the narrative provides additional and often new avenues through which an inquiry may proceed.

Chapter 8: The Analysis Process and Alternate Forms of Documentation: Transcripts
Due to the length of a transcript, the opportunities for analysis and discovery are enhanced significantly.

Chapter 9: Multiple Document Analysis Synergisms
There are circumstances wherein the sum of one-plus-one equals more than two.

Chapter 10: Deep Sentence Analysis
There is a whole world down there.

You will discover Chapters 1 through 8 contain an examination at the conclusion of each chapter.

Lastly, in investigative discourse analysis, a working knowledge of the parts of speech is imperative. For many of us it has been a while since primary school. If needed, an internet search on the parts of speech will provide a multitude of resources. Just in case.

Introduction

Question: What is investigative discourse analysis?

Answer: It is an additional examination technique for the individual having the responsibility for making inquiry and bringing that inquiry to resolution. It places a focus on the linguistic aspect of interpersonal communication. Herein investigative discourse analysis is not presented as a methodology to replace or supplant other modalities of inquiry but rather as an additional option added to the process—the idea being the more options available the greater the possibility for a positive outcome.

Though by no means is investigative discourse analysis limited to application regarding the interview process, performing an analysis prior to conducting an interview *is* the gold standard when it comes to planning for the interview. Within the arena of the interview process the guidelines are: ACE:

A - Allow the individual to provide their story;
C - Conduct the analysis;
E - Execute the interview.

The authors have long conceptualized investigative discourse analysis as "common sense with the accompanying labels and process." We have found by anchoring what is already known to the appropriate linguistic terminologies a more effective transition from "knowing" to "performing" occurs.

The following definitions can serve as the foundation of our study of investigative discourse analysis. The terms, concepts, definitions, methodologies and purposes that we acquire as we proceed through our study rest upon this foundation.

Investigative: To study closely and systematically.

Discourse: Communication, expression, or interchange of thoughts, sometimes within a *narrative*, which is a statement of real or purported events, occurrences or conditions.

Analysis: The process of separating a 'thing' into its component parts or elementary qualities.

Investigative Discourse Analysis: The close and systematic study of the basic linking components of spoken or written communication in order to determine:

Process: how something operates or is accomplished;

Occurrence: when something happened or the manner in which it happened;

Descriptions: detailed, vague or missing;

Individual(s) involved: who did what and when;

Evaluation: good/bad - right/wrong;

Relationships: consistent or changing;

Reasons for specific word selections;

To convey or convince: the form and the semantic quality of the narrative.

The Importance of Words in Investigative Discourse Analysis

Words are things. —Mirabeau

Within discourse, words serve as the smallest units of analysis. For the person who would seek to acquire the skill of analyzing discourse, there must be an accompanying fascination with words. We will have the opportunity to examine *every word* an individual uses, for each one is crucial and worthy of evaluation. Discourse analysis is comprised, to paraphrase Emerson, of "fossil words." Discourse analysis requires us to be verbal archaeologists, examining the entire wording to determine how each word fits with the other – or not.

Mirabeau was correct. Words are indeed "things." And because words are things, we can, in a sense, pick them up and examine them and their relationship to the other words which we find nearby:

- *What did the individual say?*
- *What did the individual mean to say?*
- *What do we determine the individual said?*
- *What part (if any) of the discourse was meant to convey or convince?*
- *What assists you toward making the determination?*

As Ben Jonson said, "As a man speaks, so he thinks; and as he thinketh in his heart, so is he." And therein we find the essence of investigative discourse analysis: to know the heart of the individual by the systematic analysis of what he said.

The truth really is out there. Let's go find it.

Investigative Discourse Analysis

Chapter 1

Terms, Concepts, and Definitions

Concepts addressed in this chapter

Words as signs
Me
They
I
We
My – introjections
Word choices
Abjuration terms
Explanatory terms
Words form sentences
Repression
Denial or negation
Temporal lacunas
Stalling mechanisms
Modifying or qualifying terms
False supportives
Marker words

Introduction

An imperative point to fix firmly in your mind as we begin our journey into the process and application of investigative discourse analysis is this: whenever reading a copy of a document—be it narrative, transcript, email, or letter—on which you are going to conduct analysis, do not read through quickly as if the analysis were a timed exercise. Investigative discourse analysis involves attending to and processing every word in the document as if it were a piece of trace evidence in a crime scene. Every word is important. Think of your reading as a stroll, not a sprint. Think tortoise, not hare.

Task 1

The following is the narrative taken from the interview of United States Army Captain Jeffrey MacDonald. Captain MacDonald was convicted of the murder of his pregnant wife and two daughters. Carefully read MacDonald's response. As you read, circle, note, highlight, or underline anything from his narrative that grabs your attention. Do not try and establish why you noted an element, just mark it and continue.

The next imperative of investigative discourse analysis is this: identify first; comprehend later. Only after the initial reading, with all needed subsequent workings with the document, is the license to think, ponder, and analyze granted. Keep in mind, however, that only in the third phase when we bring together the document, its analysis, and the narrator does the opportunity to know all become a possibility.

GREBNER: Just go ahead and tell us your story.

MACDONALD: Let's see. Monday night my wife went to bed, and I was reading. And I went to bed about—somewheres around two o'clock. I really don't know; I was reading on the couch, and my little girl Kristy had gone into bed with my wife. And I went in to go to bed, and the bed was wet. She had wet the bed on my side, so I brought her in her own room. And I don't remember if I changed her or not; gave her a bottle and went out to the couch 'cause my bed was wet. And I went to sleep on the couch. And then the next thing I know I heard some screaming, at least my wife; but I thought I heard Kimmie, my older daughter, screaming also. And I sat up. The kitchen light was on, and I saw some people at the foot of the bed.

So, I don't know if I really said anything or I was getting ready to say something. This happened real fast. You know, when you talk about it, it sounds like it took forever; but it didn't take forever.

And so, I sat up; and at first I thought it was—I just could see three people, and I don't know if I—If I heard the girl first—or I think I saw her first. I think two of the men separated sort of at the end of my couch, and I keep—all I saw was some people really.

And this guy started walking down between the coffee table and the couch, and he raised something over his head and just sort of then—sort of all together—I just got a glance of this girl with kind of a light on her face. I don't know if it was a flashlight or a candle, but it looked to me like she was holding something. And I just remember that my instinctive thought was that "she's holding a candle. What the hell is she holding a candle for?" But she said, before I was hit the first time, "Kill the pigs. Acid's groovy."

Now, that's all—that's all I think I heard before I was hit the first time, and the guy hit me in the head. So I was knocked back on the couch, and then I started struggling to get up, and I could hear it all then—Now I could—Maybe it's really, you know—I don't know if I was repeating to myself what she just said or if I kept hearing it, but I kept—I heard, you know, "Acid is groovy. Kill the pigs."

And I started to struggle up; and I noticed three men now; and I think the girl was kind of behind them, either on the stairs or at the foot of the couch behind them. And the guy on my left was a colored man, and he hit me again; but at the same time, you know, I was kind of struggling. And these two men, I thought, were punching me at the same time. Then I—I remember thinking to myself that—see, I work out with the boxing gloves sometimes. I was then—and I kept—"Geeze, that guy throws a hell of a punch," because he punched me in the chest, and I got this terrible pain in my chest.

And so, I was struggling, and I got hit on the shoulder or the side of the head again, and so I turned and I—and I grabbed this guy's whatever it was. I thought it was a baseball bat at the time. And I had—I was holding it. I was kind of working up it to hold onto it.

Meanwhile, both these guys were kind of hitting me, and all this time I was hearing screams. That's what I can't figure out, so—let's see, I was holding—so, I saw the—and all I got a glimpse was, was some stripes. I told you, I think, they were E6 stripes. There was one bottom rocker and it was an army jacket, and that man was a colored man, and the two men, other men, were white.

And I didn't really notice too much about them. And so I kind of struggled, and I was kind of off balance, 'cause I was still halfway on the couch and half off, and I was holding onto this thing. And I kept getting this pain, either in — you know, like sort of in my stomach, and he kept hitting me in the chest.

And so, I let go of the club; and I was grappling with him and I was holding his hand in my hand. And I saw, you know, a blade. I didn't know what it was; I just saw something that looked like a blade at the time.

And so, then I concentrated on him. We were kind of struggling in the hallway right there at the end of the couch; and then really the next distinctive thing, I thought that—I thought that I noticed that—I saw some legs, you know, that—not covered—like I'd saw the top of some boots. And I thought that I saw knees as I was falling.

But it wasn't what was in the papers that I saw white boots. I never saw white, muddy boots. I saw—saw some knees on the top of boots, and I told, I think, the investigators, I thought they were brown, as a matter of fact.

And the next thing I remember, though, was lying on the hallway floor, and I was freezing cold and it was very quiet. And my teeth were chattering, and I went down and—to the bedroom.

And I had this—I was dizzy, you know. I wasn't really—real alert; and I—my wife was lying on the—the floor next to the bed. And there were—there was a knife in her upper chest.

So, I took that out; and I tried to give her artificial respiration but the air was coming out of her chest. So, I went and checked the kids; and—just a minute—and they were—had a lot of—there was a lot of blood around.

So, I went back into the bedroom; and I—this time I was finding it real hard to breathe, and I was dizzy. So I picked up the phone and I told this asshole operator that it was—my name was Captain MacDonald and I was at 544 Castle Drive and I needed the MPs and a doctor and an ambulance. And she said, "Is this on post or off post?"—something like that.

And I started yelling at her. I said—finally, I told her it was on post, and she said, "Well, you'll have to call the MPs."

So, I dropped the phone; and I went back and I checked my wife again; and now I was—I don't know. I assume I was hoping I hadn't seen what I had seen or I'd—or I was starting to think more like a doctor. So, I went back and I checked for pulses. You know, carotid pulses and stuff; and I—there was no pulse on my wife, and I was—I felt I was getting sick to my stomach and I was short of breath, and I was dizzy and my teeth were chattering 'cause I was cold. And so I didn't know if I was going—I assumed I was going into shock because I was cold. That's one of the symptoms of shock; you start getting chills.

So, I got down on all fours; and I was breathing for a while. Then I realized that I had talked to the operator and nothing really had happened with her. But in any case, when I went back to check my wife, I then went to check the kids. And a couple times I had to—thinking that I was going into shock and not being able to breathe.

Now I—you know, when I look back, of course, it's merely a symptom, that shortness of breath. It isn't—you weren't really that bad, but that's what happens when you get a pneumothorax. You—you think you can't breathe.

And I had to get down on my hands and knees and breathe for a while, and then I went in and checked the kids and checked their pulses and stuff. And—I don't know if it was the first time I checked them or the second time I checked them, to tell you the truth; but I had all—you know, blood on my hands and I had little cuts in here, and my head hurt.

So, when I reached up to feel my head, you know, my hands were bloody. And so I—I think it was the second circuit 'cause it—by that time, I was—I was thinking better, I thought. And I went into that—I went into the bathroom right there and looked in the mirror and didn't—nothing looked wrong. I mean there wasn't really even a cut or anything.

So, I—then I went out in the hall. I couldn't breathe, so I was on my hands and knees in the hall, and I—and it kept hitting me that really nothing had been solved when I called the operator.

And so I went in and—that was in the—you know, in the middle of the hallway there. And I went the other way. I went into the kitchen, picked up that phone and the operator was on the line. My other phone had never been hung up. And she was still on the line, and she said, "Is this Captain MacDonald?" I said "Yes it is." And she said, "Just a minute." And there was some dial tones and stuff and then the sergeant came on. And he said, "Can I help you?" So I told him that I needed a doctor and an ambulance and that some people had been stabbed, and that I thought I was going to die. And he said, "They'll be right there." So, I left the phone; and I remember going back to look again. And the next thing I knew, an MP was giving me mouth-to-mouth respiration next to—next to my wife.

Now, I remember I saw—I don't know if it was the first or second trip into the bedroom to see my wife—but I saw the back door was open, but that's immaterial, I guess. That's it."

Reading Summary – MacDonald Narrative

Task 2

Answer the following.

A. List ten (10) different words or phrases that drew your attention from the reading.

1. ______
2. ______
3. ______
4. ______
5. ______
6. ______
7. ______
8. ______
9. ______
10. ______

B. What was it about each word or phrase that made it salient?

1. ______
2. ______
3. ______
4. ______

5. ______________________________

6. ______________________________

7. ______________________________

8. ______________________________

9. ______________________________

10. ______________________________

C. What is your overall evaluation of MacDonald's account of what occurred?

Investigative Discourse Analysis Terminology

Within the study of any concept, a working knowledge of the terms specific to that discipline provides the greatest advantage toward comprehension and application. Terms are like the handles on a suitcase. A suitcase with no handle has a degree of functionality, however a suitcase having a handle is a great deal more useful. Similarly, someone reading a narrative with no knowledge of the linguistic actions present in the narrative will gain some information from the reading. However, the person capable of naming and understanding the dynamics of linguistic operations will glean significantly more from the reading of the narrative. In the process of evaluating the MacDonald narrative, the terms (contained therein) which are the basic building blocks of investigative discourse analysis will be defined and identified.

Before we proceed further, two fundamental terms to investigative discourse analysis are *narrative* and *account*. The two terms will be used interchangeably throughout the text. *Narrative* as, "a story or account of events, experiences, or the like."[1] *Account* is defined as, "an oral or written description of particular events or situations."[2]

❖ Words as Signs

Each word, whether spoken or written, is a sign. Dictionary.com defines *sign* as, "any object, action, event, pattern, etc., that conveys a meaning."[3] There are many different types of signs that we can "read" and interpret. The blooming flowers indicating the onset of spring are one of the more common examples of signs which occur naturally. Certain colors at sunset indicate, to those

1. *Dictionary.com,* http:000//www.dictionary.com (July, 23, 2011)).
2. Ibid. (accessed July, 23, 2011).
3. Ibid. (accessed July, 23, 2011).

who can recognize and read them, that it is going to rain. Other sunset colors indicate clear, dry weather. But these signs are meaningful only to those who are knowledgeable about what such colors signify. Leaves changing color on the trees is another naturally occurring sign, indicating the onset of fall.

There are many examples of man-made signs as well. All we have to do is travel down an urban street to observe a myriad of signs which inform, direct, warn, prohibit, and limit our activities. In most cases, to renew our driver's license we must demonstrate an ability to read and interpret signs common to traveling on roads.

A traveler must read and interpret the traffic and road signs displayed along the road in order to reach a pre-determined destination. You, in your operation of investigative discourse analysis, must be able to read and interpret the signs (linguistic components) an individual displays within the narrative in order to reach your destination—the truth.

Within the study of discourse analysis, a sign is a linguistic unit—written or spoken—that is the symbol of an idea. To the knowledgeable analyst, these signs convey meaning and, consequently, can be interpreted. The discourse analyst is required to be versed in the science of signs, or *semiotics* as it relates to linguistic phenomena.

Words are things but words can also represent things. For example the printed or spoken word *proposal* is not the actual proposal itself, but rather a sign representing the proposal. Likewise, the name *Mary* is not actually the person, but rather a sign representing the individual who is referred to as *Mary*. Consequently, the words which form the sentence *Mary has the proposal* represent the relationship between Mary and the proposal. This sentence conveys information to those who can interpret its signs regarding the status of the proposal and Mary.

❖ Word Choices

Every word used by an individual speaker in a narrative is a matter of choice. The speaker selects each word. This selection process is a form of behavior. Behavior is directed toward the accomplishment of a goal. That goal may be to convey fully or to withhold information. As Emerson said, "Words are also actions, and actions are a kind of words." Therefore, an individual's choice of words is a form of selective action or behavior which will reveal to the analyst as much about the speaker himself as it will about whatever is being described or related.

The behavior displayed by the speaker's word selection has both a meaning and purpose. Consequently, every word and phrase in the MacDonald narrative—from "Let's see" to "That's it"—was chosen. Those choices were a form of behavior on the part of MacDonald. His behavior was directed toward the accomplishment of a goal. The goal could be to fully convey information or to convince someone that he *was*, in fact, fully conveying information.

Our analysis efforts are directed toward the determination of the meaning and primary aim of the narrative as presented by the individual. Each of these different goals—to convey or to convince—will be linked to a different set of linguistic behaviors as evidenced by (in part, but not limited to) the presenter's word selection.

If the speaker's goal is to convince, she will behave accordingly in terms of the words selected to develop the discourse. Conversely, as we will observe, an individual whose goal is to convey will behave differently in terms of word selection and narrative development.

❖ Words Form Sentences

From the smallest unit of analysis—words—we proceed to the next level of consideration, the *sentence*. A sentence is defined as, "a grammatical unit that is composed of one or more clauses."[4]

Sentences are built by the speaker, word by word. This sentence construction is itself a complicated task since the speaker has a considerable number of words from which to choose from at each point of sentence development. Additional complications arise when the mental processes of the speaker are in conflict—over whether to convey the truth or endeavor to convince the listener of their version of events, for example. When an individual is conveying information, they do not edit their narrative. Incidentals and extraneous bits of information are included. Details are provided that place the information in context and aid in understanding. When an individual has the goal of only convincing another of the veracity of their assertion they choose their words to provide only that which is minimally necessary (in their mind) to succeed.

Details, incidentals and extraneous information could serve as additional points for inquiry. Subsequently they are omitted. These diametrically opposed forces will leave informative traces, as it were, in the discourse, which the analysis can reveal.

Each word in the sentence is selected, consciously or unconsciously. The selection process is influenced by two factors: (1) the rules of the language that were assimilated by the speaker in the early stages of language acquisition; and (2) the goal of the individual (e.g., to convince or convey).

Let us return now to our examination of MacDonald's account of the murder of his wife and daughters. We will use his account as a learning vehicle as we begin to address related terms, concepts and definitions below.

The Pronoun *I*

I is the pronoun which refers to the speaker. Pay attention to the individual's use of this pronoun. Always note where the pronoun *I* is present in the narrative and where it disappears from the narrative. Pay particular attention to the content of the discourse at the point where this change occurs. The absence of the pronoun *I*, in statements such [1]as: "Went to the store," for example, may indicate the individual's loss of commitment to his own narrative or to what he is asserting at that point. A high use can indicate a degree of self-absorption.

Task 3

Review MacDonald's utilization of the pronoun *I*. How does his frequency of self-referencing relate to his references to his family?

Introjection

The use of the possessive pronoun *my* is an example of psychological introjection. Introjection is defined as, "an unconscious psychic process by which a person incorporates into his or her own psychic apparatus the characteristics of another person or object."[5] *My* refers to the speaker, or self, and indicates possession or possessiveness.

---

4. *Glossary of Linguistic Terms* http://sil.org/linguistics/GlossaryOflinguisticTerms/ (July, 23, 2011).
5. *Dictionary.com,* http://www.dictionary.com (July 23, 2011).

Task 4

In the early portion of MacDonald's narrative, note the frequency of the use of introjection. What could account for this high application?

Marker Words

The is an example of a marker word. Marker words label or otherwise foucs on the word being identified. Other examples of marker words in sentences are: "*A* fraudulent expense was in *the* request for reimbursement form"; "We returned to *her* house"; "*This* matter is something that has to be resolved"; and "*That* was a difficult period in my life." In the analysis of discourse, identify the marker words and note any changes in their usage.

In evaluating a narrative, pay attention to the use of the pronoun *me*, which is defined as, "that aspect of self that represents those components of one's total self that derive from the environment, the material possessions, the internalized social values."[6] *Me*" is the objective case of *I*. *Me* is also the most intimate of all the pronouns. Heavy use of the pronoun *me* may indicate that the individual perceives himself, or wishes to portray himself, as the passive object of external actions or events over which he has no control.

Task 5

Find all of the instances of MacDonald's utilization of the pronoun *me*. Where does the clustering or grouping of *me* occur within his account? Why do you think this clustering is manifested at this particular juncture within the narrative?

Abjuration Terms

The conjunction *but* is an example of an abjuration term. It serves to withdraw the assertion made in the previous clause of the sentence. This linguistic operation causes the second portion of the sentence (after the abjuration term) to take priority over that which came before the abjuration term. More often than not, abjuration terms are conjunctions. When someone says, "I don't want to make you mad, but," you can be sure that whatever will follow is designed to do just that.

6. Reber, Arthur S. and Emily Reber, *The Penguin Dictionary of Psychology*, 3rd ed., (Penguin 2002) s.v. "me."

Task 6

In the last paragraph of the MacDonald narrative, there are two uses of abjuration terms. Locate the two examples. Note what is said after each abjuration term. What point is MacDonald endeavoring to make?

Psychological Repression

Psychological repression is defined as, "a defense mechanism whereby unacceptable thoughts, feelings, or wishes are banished from consciousness."[7] Indications of repression will always draw the analyst's attention. When the purpose of the narrative is presumably to convey what happened and the individual reveals *he remembers there are elements that he does not remember*, that portion of the narrative merits further attention in the form of amplifying questions. In Chapter 6 we will address the amplification process.

Task 7

In the MacDonald narrative, before his articulation of the attack, there is an example of repression. Find the example.

Temporal Lacuna

A *temporal lacuna* denotes a blank space or missing element(s) within the discourse. Some portion of the narrative has been passed over or left out of the narrative. Examples of temporal lacunae are "later on," "after that," or "by and by."

Task 8

In the MacDonald narrative, there are examples of temporal lacuna transitions to articulation of the attack and subsequent actions after the attack. Locate those examples.

7. Colman, Andrew M., *Oxford Dictionary of Psychology*, 3rd ed., (Oxford University Press 2009), s.v. "psychological repression."

Modifying or Qualifying Terms

Modifying or *qualifying terms* allow the speaker to "reduce or lessen in degree or extent"[8] the force of a statement. The speaker lacks confidence in his or her own assertion, which may indicate some difficulty with committing to what is being said. Examples of modifying or qualifying terms are:

I *believe* the first time I saw him was a week ago.
I *guess* he had another account.
It was *kind of* a threat to me.
We were *sort of* waiting to update the ledgers.
Basically what happened was ...
Normally the checks are posted to the patient's account and deposited in the bank.
I *think* I posted the sale the day after the transaction.

As another example, a sports figure whose marriage had been precipitated by some legal efforts on the part of his bride was quoted as saying, "[I] *think* it's going to help me ... I can concentrate on [the sport] again and give it a *little* more 100 percent on the [field], especially practice and stuff ... I *guess* it's just love and we're going to make it work *the best we can* ... I *think* it's going to be good for me ... It's going to be good for [bride's name] too ... *Hopefully* we can live the rest of our lives together."

The analyst should note when modifying or qualifying terms appear in the discourse, particularly as a function of change.

Task 9

Read MacDonald's account of the attack. Identify all examples of the modifying or qualifying terms within this portion of his narrative. Why do you think this high clustering of modifying or qualifying terms appear at a specific point within the narrative?

Collective Referencing—The Pronoun *We*

The pronoun *we* indicates a collective reference to the writer or speaker and at least one other individual. It is an example of verbal immediacy indicating a reduced emotional and/or physical distance between persons. Within the analysis of discourse, always note the use and context of *we.*

Additionally, look for clustering of the pronoun *we.* Those who would endeavor to misdirect will manipulate things and they will manipulate people. One method of manipulating people is for the writer to place himself in the middle of the herd. A good analogy would be a zebra. The zebra is more protected in the middle of the herd—the collective *we.* In some circumstances, use of the first person pronoun *I* would be the equivalent of the zebra standing out away from the herd thus increasing the chance of being attacked by the lion. The analyst should always note when the writer transitions from the use of the first person pronoun to a clustering of the pronoun *we.*

8. *Dictionary.Reference.com*, http://www.dictionary.com (February 3, 2012).

Task 10

Locate the use of the pronoun *we* within the MacDonald narrative. Who specifically was MacDonald referencing? Giving consideration to the concept of *we* as a function of verbal immediacy, what inferences come to mind?

Psychological Distancing—The Pronoun *They*

Additionally, note the usage of the third person pronoun *they*. The pronoun *they* is the most psychologically distancing of all the pronouns. Think of the fair weather sports fan. When the team wins he proudly exclaims, "We won." When the team loses he laments, "They lost." The analyst will note when the writer endeavors to distance himself from others via the use of the pronoun *they*.

Explanatory Terms

Explanatory terms are used to give the reason for or cause of. Explanatory terms allow for the explanation of cause and effect (e.g., "I did not write a check *since* Jimmy had given me the money."), justification, or rationale ("I left her at the dance *because* she wanted to stay."). Other examples of explanatory terms are, *so* and *therefore*.

Task 11

Review MacDonald's narrative of his actions after the attack. What explanatory term is highly represented in this portion? Why do you think MacDonald endeavored so arduously to explain his actions? Next, review MacDonald's account of what occurred before the attack. What is the level of explanatory terms within this element? Why do you think this is the case? Lastly, review his articulation of the attack itself. What is the level of explanatory terms within this element? Why do you think this is the case? Summarize MacDonald's allocation of explanatory terms throughout his narrative.

Denial or Negation

Denial, or *negation,* is defined as, "a defense mechanism involving a disavowal or failure to consciously acknowledge thoughts, feelings, desires, or aspects of reality that would be painful or unacceptable."[9] Denial or negation will be presented within the narrative when the speaker voluntarily relates what *did not* happen or what she *did not* know, *did not* do, or *did not* observe. This phenomenon is particularly striking when the speaker, having been asked to relate what happened or

9. Colman, Andrew M., *Oxford Dictionary of Psychology*, 3rd ed., (Oxford University Press 2009), s.vv. "denial," "negation."

how something is accomplished (process), proceeds to relate what did not happen or what is (or was not) not involved in a process as well. For example, an individual who was asked to describe the process wherein a contract was awarded to a company having a bid higher than other submissions wrote:

> *Once the services needed were determined, the contract went to HR and Legal for review. Next, the contract was advertised for bid submission. Once the bid submission deadline passed there was a pre-bid opening meeting with all those who had made submissions. I did not indicate to anyone that I would ensure they received the contract.*

Task 12

Review the portion of the MacDonald narrative that deals with all that occurred before the attack. Find an example of denial or negation. Why would MacDonald select this point in his narrative to engage in denial or negation linguistic behavior?

Stalling Mechanisms

Stalling mechanisms allow the speaker to hold back or pause, especially when in doubt. The most consistent characteristic of stalling mechanisms is that they are a function of change. Stalling mechanisms can be illustrated by a wide variety of linguistic factors: pauses within or between sentences, abrupt onset of stuttering or stammering, and the use of such terms as *okay now*, *well*, *oh well*,, *let's see*, or *um, ah, uh*.

Task 13

Review the MacDonald narrative for examples of stalling mechanisms. Pay attention to the content of the narrative around these examples.

False Supportives

There may be times when the speaker feels the need for additional (but unnecessary) support for what he has asserted. That need for additional support can manifest itself through the use of a *false supportive*. Examples include:

> *I swear to God.*
> *On my mother's grave.*
> *To tell you the truth.*
> *As a matter of fact.*

Task 14

Review the MacDonald narrative for examples of a false supportive. Pay attention to the content of the narrative around these examples.

Task 15

Review the list of words or phrases you picked out after your initial reading. How many of those words or phrases matched the terms we addressed in this chapter?

If you selected elements we have not addressed to this point, take heart. We are not finished with the MacDonald narrative. There are, contained within the narrative, additional terms, concepts, and definitions we will discover as we progress.

Summary

In this chapter we have addressed a series of investigative discourse analysis concepts.

By identifying and applying the terms and their definitions to the text, we have discovered there is a great deal more to be learned from discourse than a cursory reading will reveal. While there is much more material to be covered in the following chapters, familiarity with the parts of speech and the requisite terminology of discourse analysis is a critical first step on the path to conducting an analysis.

Examination

The following examination contains 29 chapter-related items. Items 1–15 require matching terms, definitions, and concepts. Items 16–25 require labeling the identified linguistic dynamic within a narrative. Items 26–29 require the identification of the linguistic dynamic found in a quote.

Items 1–15

In the space beside each numbered term, fill in the letter corresponding to the correct definition or information.

____ 1. *I*

____ 2. Marker word

____ 3. Temporal lacuna

____ 4. Modifying or qualifying term

____ 5. Explanatory term

____ 6. Denial or negation

____ 7. Stalling mechanism

____ 8. False supportive

____ 9. *We*

____10. Introjection

____11. *Me*

____12. Abjuration term

____13. Words

____14. Sign

____15. Repression

A. The smallest units of analysis

B. Any linguistic unit that is the symbol of an idea

C. An unconscious psychic process by which a person incorporates into his or her own psychic apparatus the characteristics of another person or object

D. The most intimate pronoun

E. Label or otherwise focus on a word

F. The pronoun that refers to the speaker

G. Serves to withdraw the assertion made in the previous clause of the sentence

H. Indicative or a blank space or missing element(s) within the discourse

I. A defense mechanism whereby unacceptable thoughts, feelings, or wishes are banished from consciousness

J. Allows the speaker reduce or lessen in degree or extent his or her commitment

K. A collective reference to the writer or speaker and at least one other individual

L. Gives the reason for or cause of

M. A defense mechanism involving a disavowal or failure to consciously acknowledge thoughts, feelings, desires or aspects of reality that would be painful or unacceptable

N. Allows the speaker to hold back, especially in doubt

O. Indicative of speaker's need for additional (but unnecessary) support for what he has asserted

Items 16–25

In the following portion of MacDonald's narrative, you will find numbers by bolded specific terms or phrases. Identify the term or phrase by the corresponding number.

16. ______________________ 21. ______________________

17. ______________________ 22. ______________________

18. ______________________ 23. ______________________

19. ______________________ 24. ______________________

20. ______________________ 25. ______________________

Let's see.(16) Monday night **my (17)** wife went to bed, and I was reading. And I went to bed about—somewheres around two o'clock. I really **don't know (18)**; I was reading on the couch, and my little girl Kristy had gone into bed with my wife.

And I went in to go to bed, and the bed was wet. She had wet the bed on my side, **so (19)** I brought her in her own room. And I **don't remember (20)** if I changed her or not; gave her a bottle and went out to the couch 'cause my bed was wet. And I went to sleep on the couch.

And then the next thing I know (21) I heard some screaming, at least my wife; **but (22)** I thought I heard Kimmie, my older daughter, screaming also. And I sat up. The kitchen light was on, and I saw some people at the foot of the bed.

So, I don't know if I really said anything or I was getting ready to say something. **This (23)** happened real fast. You know, when you talk about it, it sounds like it took forever; but it didn't take forever.

And so, I sat up; and at first I thought it was—I just could see three people, and I don't know if I—If I heard the girl first—or I think I saw her first. I think two of the men separated **sort of (24)** at the end of my couch, and I keep—all I saw was some people really.

And this guy started walking down between the coffee table and the couch, and he raised something over his head and just sort of then—sort of all together—I just got a glance of this girl with kind of a light on her face. I don't know if it was a flashlight or a candle, but it looked to me like she was holding something. And I just remember that my instinctive thought was that she's holding a candle. What the hell is she holding a candle for? But she said, before I was hit the first time, "Kill the pigs. Acid's groovy."

Now, that's all—that's all I think I heard before I was hit the first time, and the guy hit me in the head. So I was knocked back on the couch, and then I started struggling to get up, and I could hear it all then—Now I could—Maybe it's really, you know—I don't know if I was repeating to myself what she just said or if I kept hearing it, but I kept—I heard, you know, "Acid is groovy. Kill the pigs."

And I started to struggle up; and I noticed three men now; and I think the girl was kind of behind them, either on the stairs or at the foot of the couch behind them. And the guy on my left was a colored man, and he hit me again; but at the same time, you know, I was kind of struggling. And these two men, I thought, were punching me at the same time. Then I—I remember thinking to myself that—see, I work out with the boxing gloves sometimes. I was then—and I kept—"Geeze, that guy throws a hell of a punch," because he punched me in the chest, and I got this terrible pain in my chest.

And so, I was struggling, and I got hit on the shoulder or the side of the head again, and so I turned and I—and I grabbed this guy's whatever it was. I thought it was a baseball bat at the time. And I had—I was holding it. I was kind of working up it to hold onto it.

Meanwhile, both these guys were kind of hitting me, and all this time I was hearing screams. That's what I can't figure out, so—let's see, I was holding—so, I saw the—and all I got a glimpse was, was some stripes. I told you, I think, they were E6 stripes. There was one bottom rocker and it was an army jacket, and that man was a colored man, and the two men, other men, were white.

And I didn't really notice too much about them. And so I kind of struggled, and I was kind of off balance, 'cause I was still halfway on the couch and half off, and I was holding onto this thing. And I kept getting this pain, either in—you know, like sort of in my stomach, and he kept hitting me in the chest.

And so, I let go of the club; and I was grappling with him and I was holding his hand in my hand. And I saw, you know, a blade. I didn't know what it was; I just saw something that looked like a blade at the time.

And so, then I concentrated on him. We were kind of struggling in the hallway right there at the end of the couch; and then really the next distinctive thing, I thought that—I thought that I noticed that—I saw some legs, you know, that—not covered—like I'd saw the top of some boots. And I thought that I saw knees as I was falling.

But it wasn't what was in the papers that I saw white boots. I never saw white, muddy boots. I saw—saw some knees on the top of boots, and I told, I think, the investigators, I thought they were brown, **as a matter of fact (25)**.

Items 26–29

Identify the following:

26. A husband returns from a business trip. As he greets his wife he exclaims, "The flights were on time, the hotel was great, I closed the deal and I did not go out with another woman." What linguistic dynamic is found in that sentence?

Answer: ____.

27. A husband returns from a business trip. As he greets his wife he exclaims, "The flights were on time, the hotel was great, I closed the deal, and I don't remember if I went out with another woman." What linguistic dynamic is found in that sentence?

Answer: ____.

28. An individual states, "This is my house and my car. I have my checking account at Acme bank. My credit score is high and my savings account is well beyond the national average." These two sentences display a high usage of ______________________________.

29. An individual making reference to her son states, "Just because they do some things bad doesn't mean you are going to hate them or hurt them intentionally." The word that indicates she has relegated her son to a more distant status is __________________________.

Chapter 2

Obtaining the Individual's Narrative

Concepts addressed in this chapter

Obtaining the Individual's Narrative
Questions to Use in Eliciting a Narrative

Introduction

Obtaining the narrative appropriate for analysis can be elicited in several ways:

- *Have the person write his or her own narrative or account;*
- *Record the person's narrative and have it transcribed word for word;*
- *Write the person's dictated account yourself.*

The method of choice is to have the individual write his or her narrative of events. This narrative can be produced by the individual at home or elsewhere before being signed and delivered to the analyst. If the individual later becomes a suspect, this option can perhaps help to minimize the possibility of a claim of having been told what to write or intimidation since his account will have been written at home.

With respect to legal parameters relating to obtaining the narrative or questions pertaining to the individual's legal rights, such issues are, for the most part, local procedural considerations. Analysts should consult with judicial officials, human resources, or legal advisors in their jurisdiction or organization for guidance on how to handle any local particulars—if any—that might apply to the narrative and the circumstances under which it was obtained and utilized.

It will not adversely affect the analysis or the investigative process if the individual writes his narrative very carefully, deliberately, or selectively. No matter how the individual writes his narrative, it will be functional as an item of linguistic behavior for analysis. This behavior will reveal insight into the motivation of the person, assisting the analyst in the search for the truth. The point is not whether the individual is careful, deliberate, or selective. The point is how the analysis or the narrative will transition into the interview process.

Taking down the individual's dictated account is the most challenging way to obtain a narrative. With practice, however, the analyst can become adept at writing the individual's narrative. If the individual cannot or will not write the narrative and the possibility of recording and transcribing it is not available, then the analyst must personally write the narrative, word for word, including pauses, hesitations, and incomplete sentences. After several sessions of writing the narrative personally, the analyst's skill at encouraging the individual to write the narrative will have improved dramatically.

Questions to Use in Eliciting a Narrative

It is important that this phase of the analysis process be conducted appropriately. Improper operation at this point will have adverse effects in the second Analysis Phase and, subsequently, the third phase—Amplification. The analyst should begin the process with an *open-ended, non-specific question.* At this point in the process, the analyst is endeavoring to obtain as much information as possible from the person about:

- what happened;
- a process;
- a relationship and an understanding of what the individual is willing or able to tell.

Think of this phase of the process as looking through a magnifying glass. The goal is to obtain an adequate amount of information suitable for analysis. If the responding narrative is too short—four or five sentences—explain to the individual that you need a complete account and that the short narrative will not suffice. The narrator will at this point provide a longer, more adequate account. Be sure to review and keep the first narrative, however. Examples of open, non-specific questions are:

- *How does your billing system operate?*
- *Please explain the process for reconciling the account.*
- *What happened?*
- *What happened Saturday from the time you went to work until you went to bed?*
- *What happened when you were robbed?*

If the questions are too specific, the individual's responses will be specific as well, rather than including whatever the individual would have related if left to his own word selection and other narrating behavior.

- *Do not supplement your open-ended questions with specifics, no matter how hard the individual presses you for that structure.*

The following examples are of open-ended, nonspecific questions and the narratives obtained as a result.

Task 1

As you examine the question and the following narrative you will find words and phrases in bold print with a number. At the end of the narrative, identify the appropriate term or phrase by the corresponding number.

Question: What happened when you were injured?

Response: Uh ... on October the 8th, uh ... Paul Smith had came to **my (1)** residence uh ...that address there on Route 1, and he asked me to fix **uh ... (2)** electrical problem that uh ... was occurring with **his (3)** headlight on his car. So uh ... I told him I'd be there in around 10 minutes ... 20 minutes. **So (4)** I got there, and knocked on his trailer door. Got the key to his automobile and went to proceed to his car to check the headlight and first I went to the front. I pulled the headlights out of the car. Then I went in the car '**cause (5)** I seen there was a problem with his headlight. I went in the car and I went under the dash of the car where the electrical wiring and everything, and I started unscrewing the bottom of the dash. Then I pulled out the electrical and I took the relay switch out, which that sits on the top of the left-hand side**. So (6)** I had to come, what you could say, from the driver side and lay my head on the passenger side to go up here to get another switch wire to relay them together. And I was laying in the automobile on the floor of the automobile with my legs out the car. And I **don't really know (7)** what happened on the inside of the house, **but (8)** Mr. Smith came and the door slammed. At that time I didn't know it was him. I probably thought it was one of the kids or something. And it hit my left ankle and I twisted it with the door. And then being that he seen that the door didn't close all the way slam, he said, "Oh man, I didn't know you was in the car", and that's ... that's **basically (9)** it right there.

Place the name of appropriate term in the corresponding blank.

1. ____________________
2. ____________________
3. ____________________
4. ____________________
5. ____________________
6. ____________________
7. ____________________
8. ____________________
9. ____________________

Task 2

In addition to evaluating the question asked to produce the narrative, you will find a series of questions related to the content of the narrative. Answer the questions.

Question: Go back and tell me in your own words what you remember of this accident?

Response: Basically, I was, um ... I was getting off that day and I had called Smith Cab Company, and Mr. Jones had picked me up and I was going to 4511 Trail Road. And which he was taking me home. So I guess he figured that would be the shorter way to take me because of the traffic which I didn't know. I had just moved here in Raleigh, so he was taking me on Tarboro Road. He was going north on Tarboro Road. And this other vehicle and which was on Martin Street, making a turn and somehow she ran the red light. Our light was green, green for us to go and maybe she was trying to run ... maybe she was trying to ... you know. I guess she had ... she may have had the yellow light, but the one light had already got off to a red light and which she ... her time. It was green in our lane so basically, he was unable to stop. Then we had a collision. The impact was on the driver's side. Cause him ... you know ... trying to stop, putting on brakes real hard and which I had ... you know, injured my neck. And my back.

Answer the following questions based on your reading of the narrative above:

1. The first example of a modifying term found in the narrative is ____________________.
2. The first example of a hesitation form found in the narrative is ____________________.
3. The first example of a marker word found in the narrative is ____________________.
4. The first example of the most intimate pronoun is found after the verb ____________.
5. The first example of an explainer is found before the pronoun ____________________.
6. The first example of denial comes after the pronoun _________________________.
7. Example(s) of introjection is (are) found __________ time(s) in the narrative.

Task 3

In addition to evaluating the question asked to produce the following narrative, identify and write an example of a word or phrase found in the narrative next to the analysis term.

Question: If you would, go back to the 10th of August, and tell what you remember as best you can about the accident?

Response: Um-kay, um, on approx ... uh at approximately 10 o'clock maybe 10:15 uh p.m. that evening Linda, myself, her mother and my daughter, my 9 year old ... um stopped at a store at the corner of Trinity and Avondale? And Linda was driving, my daughter Tish, was on the passenger side in the front. I was on the driver side in the rear and um ... Linda's mom, Mrs. Smith, was on the passenger side in the rear. Um ... Linda got out to go inside the store and there was a pick up truck parked beside us ... um driven by ... um I can't remember her name. She told us then, but it's been a while. Um ... she backed ... she got in the truck, came out of the store, got in the truck and started to back out. When she backed out, she pulled forward into the right to go to leave the parking lot of the store. There's a slope sort of a slope type hill ... um and she stopped at the top of there. I assume to check and see wh ... if anything was coming or not. But, the truck started to back up instead of pulling out and she just backed in ... backed into us on the um ... passenger side. Um, she bumped us and the truck rested up against the um the back door and tire area of um the bumper of the truck did of the car that we were in. And I ... Linda was coming of the store then and there was a gentleman on the telephone and he kept saying she started to pull off is what happened. And ... and Linda and the gentleman that was standing at uh at the telephone booth said, hold it, hold it you hit 'em, you hit 'em. And she put the car, she, she put the truck, she pulled off a little bit, a little ways and put the truck in park and got out and came over to the um to the car and asked if everybody was all right. And, at that time, I got out and went around to um the rear of the car and she asked if I was all right and I told her I thought so. And Diana Smith side was the side she had hit and she was just sitting there and um Linda came around and they exchanged information. And Linda asked her, you know, if she was insured and she said yes. And Linda told her she was also, and that if um no more damage that what was done to the ca ... to the vehicle itself ... Linda asked if she wanted to just go ahead and exchange in ... um insurance information. So, s ... she said no, she ... ra ... she'd feel safer with calling the police and getting a police report done. So, um, I went and called and then when the police officer arrived, they uh traded information at that point. And then he called for back-up for some reason. I don ... I don't know exactly what was happening. But a ... another police officer did come out. And a tow truck came out. And while the officer was, the first officer, was talking to Linda, um, the other officer pulled in. And one was talking to the lady who was driving the pick up truck and the tow truck and then he told them to go ahead and that everything was all right. And the other officer asked us um if we had gotten her insurance information and she said ... she said yes. That was the end of it at that point.

Fill in the following.

1. Introjection: ______________________________
2. Marker word: ______________________________
3. Abjuration terms: ______________________________
4. Repression: ______________________________
5. Temporal lacunae: ______________________________

6. Modifying or qualifying term: ________________________________

7. Explanatory terms: ________________________________

8. Denial or negation: ________________________________

9. Stalling mechanism: ________________________________

Task 4

Keeping in mind your particular professional responsibilities, write five open, non-specific questions that would be applicable for producing a narrative of a suitable length for conducting an analysis.

1. ________________________________

2. ________________________________

3. ________________________________

4. ________________________________

5. ________________________________

Summary

In this segment, we have examined criteria for the initiating question designed to produce a broad-based narrative suitable for analysis. No phase of the process is more important than this initial phase. Failure to successfully navigate this element can readily result in adverse downstream consequence for the phase two analysis and the subsequent phase three amplification.

Examination

1. The most appropriate type of question to use in obtaining the individual's narrative is:

   ________________________________.

2. An employee has reported that the folder containing proprietary information has been duplicated. Write an appropriate question designed to obtain a narrative suitable for conducting an analysis. ________________________________.

3. A husband has reported that his missing wife never returned from her trip to the store. Write an appropriate question designed to obtain a narrative suitable for conducting an analysis.

   ________________________________.

4. Evaluate the applicability of the following for obtaining a narrative suitable for analysis: "Please write out what happened during the shooting, including who did what and what you saw and heard." ____________________

____

____

5. Evaluate the applicability of the following for obtaining a narrative suitable for analysis: "Tell me about the missing money." ____________________

____

____

6. The following is a narrative regarding a vehicle accident. You have been tasked with presenting a briefing on the linguistic elements (presented to this point) found within the narrative. Prepare for the briefing in a manner you find suitable to demonstrate your ability to locate and articulate the linguistic elements found therein.

> My wife and I and a family friend were going to downtown, about 10:45 p.m. Got to junction of Jamestown Road and Dark Forest Road. And suddenly what I saw was a truck, a moving truck come onto the road. It was so spontaneous I cannot graphically begin to tell you what happened. But it was so spontaneous that by the time I saw the truck and applied my brakes ... It was on a slope. Rather the truck was standing on a slope, because the Jamestown Road slopes this way. And by the time I saw it, it had already hit the front, the front light. And I applied my brakes and I attempted to swerve to the left. By the time I could bring the car to a halt, it had gone all the way down the length you just saw. It took awhile for me to regain composure. My wife was sitting next to me. The impact jolted her toward my direction. As soon as I had gotten composure, I looked in the back and asked my friend "Are you okay?" He did not respond immediately and I came out of the car and I walked out, to go, to see if I could get a phone to call the police.

Chapter 3

Analysis of Narrative by Its Form

Concepts addressed in this chapter

Structural Analysis of the narrative
Narrative Alignment
Identifying the Formal Organization of the narrative
- Before: *subordinate information* (SI) — the prologue
- During: *central issue* (CI) — the event
- After: *subordinate information* (SI) — the epilogue

Determining the Central Issue
Subjective Time Allocation

Introduction

Many of the participants in our classes have found identifying the form of the narrative to be the most challenging component of the analysis process. It does not have to be. Oddly enough, this is the portion of the analysis process wherein a lack of experience can be an asset. Here is what transpires: experienced personnel can have a tendency to think through the narrative in addition to and in conjunction with the process of conducting the analysis. They draw upon their experiences and endeavor to quickly determine *what really happened.* At that point, confirmation bias runs onto the playground and investigative discourse analysis runs off. The two will never play together. The analyst can't hold fast to a theory and conduct an analysis simultaneously. When the analyst has, in his mind, reached the *Aha* of the matter, he will only see elements which confirm his belief and dismiss elements which may point to the contrary. Make sure this does not happen to you.

A participant lacking experience is a particular area — homicide, for example — has an inclination to simply detect what is there. They have no similar experiences for which to frame a reference and from which to jump to conclusions. That is the key at this point in the analysis. The analyst should simply detect and process. Do not jump to a conclusion. The potential to gain full knowledge resides at stage three.

From the initial reading of the document through the development of the amplifying questions (stage three) the analyst should have a mindset of *what is there is what is there.* In this manner, when discovering a related linguistic component the analyst can think along these lines:

> *Okay. I have found a salient component in the narrative. I am not ready to state any reason as to why the component is present. I see the presence of this component as an opportunity to formulate a related question once I interview the person based on my analysis. There is all likelihood the interviewee will be able to respond to the question I pose and bring that component*

to a satisfactory resolution. If that is not the case then the interviewee will be faced with the challenge of confronting his own words, increasing my opportunity to learn still more from the conduct of the interview.

The analysis of discourse consists of a "rich interpretation" which is an "extended and expanded interpretation of a text, a discourse ... that brings to bear all that is known about the ... persons involved and ... the processes under examination."[1]

Narrative Alignments

There are two alignments of the narrative along which the analysis is conducted:

1. the structure or form of the narrative;
2. the semantics (meaning) of the words used in the narrative.

The analyst initially seeks to determine the structure or form of the narrative. In the analysis of linguistic behavior involving documents other than narratives, i.e., transcripts, emails, letters, etc., the structure or form will not be an operational factor. With non-narrative document types, the semantic analysis will be the primary focus.

Next, the analyst will conduct a semantic analysis of the narrative. The semantic analysis will suggest any specific points where inaccuracies or a lack of clarity may be present, as well as those points where the interviewee will be afforded the opportunity to amplify or expand upon his/her narrative. (Chapter 4 will address the process of semantic analysis.)

Identifying the Formal Organization of the Narrative

The narrative's formal organization should be reviewed in terms of *uniformity*. The individual's narrative concerns an event which has occurred in the past, and the person has provided the narrative in response to an appropriate open-ended question. Therefore, we would expect to be able to identify those narrative units that indicate what happened:

- before: *subordinate information* (SI)—the prologue;
- during: *central issue* (CI)—the event;
- after: *subordinate information* (SI)—the epilogue.

Task 1

Refer back to the MacDonald narrative in Chapter 1. Notice how he delineated his account by telling what happened before the attack, during the attack, and after the attack. Find the points within his narrative where he made the transitions. What linguistic component is found at each transitional point?

Answer: ____

____

____

1. Reber, Arthur S. and Emily Reber, *The Penguin Dictionary of Psychology*, 3rd ed., (Penguin 2002).

This breakdown of the narrative into three basic components is most definitely not a modern discovery. The following is a passage from Aristotle's *Poetics*, written around 350 B.C.:

> [The plot describes] an action that is complete, and whole, and of a certain magnitude; for there may be a whole that is wanting in magnitude. A whole is that which has a beginning, a middle, and an end. A beginning is that which does not itself follow anything by causal necessity, but after which something naturally is or comes to be. An end, on the contrary, is that which itself naturally follows some other thing, either by necessity, or as a rule, but has nothing following it. A middle is that which follows something as some other thing follows it. A well constructed plot, therefore, must neither begin nor end at haphazard, but conform to these principles.[2]

Now if we can be so presumptuous as to paraphrase Aristotle and work his conception into a perspective more applicable to investigative discourse analysis:

> A **narrative** is complete, and whole, and of a certain magnitude; for there may be a **portion of the narrative** that is wanting in magnitude. A whole is that which has a beginning (**SI**,) a middle (**CI**), and an end (**SI**). A beginning (**before—SI**) is that which does not itself follow anything by causal necessity, but after which something (**during—CI**) naturally is or comes to be. An end (**after—SI**) on the contrary, is that which itself naturally follows some other thing, either by necessity, or as a rule, but has nothing following it. A middle (**during—CI**) is that which follows something as some other thing follows it. A well constructed **narrative**, therefore, must neither begin nor end haphazardly, but conform to these principles.

Always note the starting point of the narrative as provided by the teller of the tale. As Aristotle related, narratives "neither begin nor end at haphazard" points. There is a linking of the individual's narrative starting point with the central issue. For example, in our focus on the MacDonald narrative, we would contemplate the following questions: "Why would MacDonald begin his account with his daughter having wet the bed?" "How, in his mind, is the daughter wetting the bed linked to the home invasion and the subsequent assault and homicide?"

Answer: ______________________________

____

____

The critical question with regard to the form of the narrative is: "Is there uniformity of linguistic time spent (known as subjective time) among the prologue (SI), the event (CI), and the epilogue (SI) sections of the narrative?" Subjective time is the amount of time as shown by the word count in a sentence, the total number of words in a unit of the narrative, and the total words the narrator utilizes to tell the story.

2. http://classics.mit.edu/Aristotle/poetics.html 29 July 2011.

For example, in the MacDonald narrative:

- Total word count of the narrative is 1,784 words (to determine the percentage breakdown in the units of narrative the analyst must first obtain the total word count in the narrative);
- Total word count for the beginning (SI—Prologue) is 107 words;
- Breakdown of the word count for the nine sentences in the prologue:

Sentence 1	2 words
Sentence 2	11 words
Sentence 3	10 words
Sentence 4	4 words
Sentence 5	18 words
Sentence 6	13 words
Sentence 7	16 words
Sentence 8	25 words
Sentence 9	8 words

A narrative that is significantly lacking in uniformity of the application of subjective time is of particular note to the analyst. The individual can misdirect by leaving something out of his narrative or by adding actions, conversations, or events which did not in fact occur during the incident. When this manipulation of reality occurs, the uniformity of the narrative can be affected. For example, if something is omitted, that section of the narrative can be truncated, whereas if something is added, that section may be disproportionately expanded.

In either case, the form of the narrative will be a factor for evaluation. Similarly, when an individual provides specific details in one section of the narrative, but fills another section with vague generalizations, the narrative uniformity can once more affected, and this lack of uniformity will become apparent to the analyst.

Our guarded reactions to narrative imbalance have a long tradition. In the second book of Maccabees, chapter 2, verse 32, found in the Apocrypha, we read "it is a foolish thing to make a long prologue and to be short in the story itself."[3]

As we shall see, sometimes it is the epilogue that is too long in relation to the central issue or the prologue. Additionally, either the prologue or the epilogue, or both, may be missing entirely. For example:

> I was gone to carry my father to the store. When I got back I saw the car was already burned down when I arrived. The fireman was there and I talked to the Fire Chief. He asked me if the car had tags. I told him "yes." He said the tag must have caught on fire. He asked for the registration card and I gave it to him.

In the above, for all practical purposes, there is only the central issue in the narrative.

Each of these types of narrative imbalance can provide the analyst with information and direction. Heraclitus, the Greek philosopher, said, "Everything flows." And so it is with a narrative. The event, as narrated by the individual, should *flow* from beginning to end. There is a certain course the narrative should follow. Any deviation from that course will be noticed by the analyst and will merit further examination.

3. http://www.kingjamesbibleonline.org/1611_2-Maccabees-2-32/ 5 August 2011.

Determining the Central Issue

Fundamental to determining the form of the narrative is the ability to locate the beginning and end of the central issue.

To determine the central issue or event of the narrative, the analyst considers:

- *What is the essential or principal element of the narrative?*
- *What is the element that endows everything else in the narrative with meaning or purpose?*
- *What is this narrative about?*
- *If this narrative is about X, at what point does X enter the narrative?*

The following narrative examples will serve to illustrate the relationships between the central issue and the secondary elements of a narrative. This first narrative deals with a vehicle accident.

> On July 18th, 1969, at approximately 11:15 P.M. in Chappaquiddick, Martha's Vineyard, Massachusetts, I was driving my car on Main Street on my way to get the ferry back to Edgartown. I was unfamiliar with the road and turned right onto Dike Road, instead of bearing hard left on Main Street. After proceeding for approximately one-half mile on Dike Road I descended a hill and came upon a narrow bridge.

Everything the teller of the tale describes happening *before* the car went off of the bridge comprises the *prologue*. This portion contains the initial *subordinate information* (SI) of the narrative.

> The car went off the side of the bridge. There was one passenger with me, one Miss ______, a former secretary of my brother Sen. Robert Kennedy. The car turned over and sank into the water and landed with the roof resting on the bottom.

Everything the individual describes in the second portion above happened *during* the period when the car went off the bridge and sank. This portion comprises the event, or *central issue* (CI) of the narrative. The central issue is the key element, the main event, the focal point of the narrative. The car going off of the bridge is the beginning of the central issue. Had the car not gone off the bridge, everything else related in this narrative would either not have happened (after the CI) or not have mattered (before the CI).

> I attempted to open the door and the window of the car but have no recollection of how I got out of the car. I came to the surface and then repeatedly dove down to the car in an attempt to see if the pas-

> senger was still in the car. I was unsuccessful in the attempt. I recall walking back to where my friends were eating. There was a car parked in front of the cottage and I climbed into the backseat. I then asked for someone to bring me back to Edgartown. I remember walking around for a period then going back to my hotel room. When I fully realized what had happened this morning, I immediately contacted the police.

Everything the individual describes happening *after* the car went off the bridge and sank comprises the *epilogue*, which contains the second set of *subordinate information* of the narrative. Consequently, the formal, subjective time, proportions of the narrative are distributed as follows:

- *Prologue*: (30% of the narrative) 70 words
- *Event*: (19% of the narrative) 45 words
- *Epilogue*: (51% of the narrative) 121 words

Alternatively, the subjective time allocation of the narrative can be illustrated as follows:

- Prologue (SI) ————————————
- Event (CI) ————————
- Epilogue (SI) ————————————————————

As a result of the structural imbalance, this narrative is described has having a **Disproportional Subjective Time Allocation** (DSTA).

Just because the narrative is determined to have a disproportional subjective time allocation does not mean we are now ready to summarily declare the individual providing the narrative as deceptive or the doer of a wrongful deed. All we can assert with confidence is that the narrative lacks uniformity with regard to the allocation of subjective time.

Let's examine another narrative. This narrative deals with the allegation of a sexual assault:

> I had been at a party for approx. 3 hours when I had to go to the bathroom. As I was walking to the bathroom I started talking to this girl because we had to wait in line. She was looking a little drunk but so was I. She went into the bathroom and when she opened the door to exit I quickly ran past her in a hurry to use the bathroom.

Within this narrative, everything that occurred before the sexual encounter is contained in the above. This portion constitutes the prologue. (Before) (SI)

> As I was using the toilet I noticed that she was still in there. When I was finished she started to rub my chest. I then ask her her name and she told me. We started to kiss and she fell onto the bathroom floor. We continued to kiss then she started rubbing my crotch. So I began to do the same to her. I continued to rub her then I inserted my middle finger into her vagina. She said she was a virgin so I didn't continue for too long. By that time people were banging on the door so I got off the floor. She then started to suck my penis but only for a few seconds. I then helped her up off the floor. We straightened up our clothes and then proceeded to exit the bathroom.

All that the individual related about the sexual encounter is contained in this segment. This portion constitutes the event (During) (CI). As this portion comprises the central issue or event of the narrative, the sexual encounter is framed by the other actions and events in the narrative.

> When we left the bathroom some of my friends and other people were outside the door waiting to use the bathroom. I walked up the steps and she sat down on the steps and was talking to another guy. (Davy Jones?) I left the party shortly afterwards and was gone for about 30 minutes. When I got back all the people were asking me what happened. I didn't even know what they were talking about until someone said this girl claims I raped her. I then was approached by 2 guys that I didn't know. They asked me if I had been with this girl and I said "yes we messed around in the bathroom." I started to walk away when he hit me on the top of my head. Then a large fight broke out. The police arrived and it was over.

All that the individual related about what happened after the sexual encounter is contained in this last segment. This last segment constitutes the epilogue (After) (SI). Consequently, the formal proportions of the narrative are distributed as follows:

Task 2

Fill in the blanks:

Prologue: (____% of the narrative) _____ words

Event: (____% of the narrative) _____ words

Epilogue: (____% of the narrative) _____ words

Alternatively, the narrative can be diagrammed as follows:

Task 3

Diagram the narrative allocation of subjective time:

Before:

During:

After:

Task 4

As a result of the structural imbalance, this narrative is described as having a (choose one):

_____ Proportional subjective time allocation (PSTA)

_____ Disproportional subjective time allocation (DSTA)

Task 5

Try your hand at identifying the beginning and end of the central issue. In our text, as in our classes, you will never lose points for trying.

> On the day of August 17, 20__, I with Gene Smith drove to a grocery store and parked outside in the parking lot. We sat for 20 minutes watching the store. When there was no more than 2 customers in there me and Gene left the car and went into the store. After we were in the store I went toward the back of the store while Gene got in the checkout line. When Gene reached the checkout girl, he pulled a pistol out and shouted, "this is a stick-up." This was my signal to come back up front. Upon getting there Gene told the checkout girl to open the cash register. After she had it open, I grabbed a paper bag and stuffed the money into the bag. Before leaving the store, I locked the cashier and the meat market man into the freezer.

> We left the store, got into a green truck, fled down main street, made a wrong turn on a one-way street. That's when the police officer seen us. we tried to outrun the patrol car, lost control, and hit a telephone pole. That is when they caught us with the money and weapons.

Answer the following:

I would begin the central issue with the sentence: ______________________________

____.

I would end the central issue with the sentence: ______________________________

____.

My rationale for this framing of the central issue is: ____________________________

____.

Task 6

Now compare your selections with the following.

> On the day of August 17, 19__, I with Gene Smith drove to a grocery store and parked outside in the parking lot. We sat for20 minutes watching the store. When there was no more than 2 customers in there me and Gene left the car and went into the store. After we were in the store I went toward the back of the store while Gene got in the checkout line.

This segment of the narrative comprises the prologue, or everything that happened before the robbery. All of the above could have occurred and there would still have not been a robbery.

> When Gene reached the checkout girl, he pulled a pistol out and shouted, "this is a stick-up." This was my signal to come back up front. Upon getting there Gene told the checkout girl to open the cash register. After she had it open, I grabbed a paper bag and stuffed the money into the bag. Before leaving the store, I locked the cashier and the meat market man into the freezer.

These sentences contain all that was related about the robbery itself. This segment is the central issue or event of the narrative. Once Gene pulled the pistol and declared the robbery there was no going back. This articulated action is the pivotal point—the defining moment. It is the equivalent of the car going off the bridge in one of the previous narratives we examined. The analyst strives to find the pivotal point—the portion wherein the teller of the tale first gets to the point.

> We left the store, got into a green truck, fled down main street, made a wrong turn on a one-way street. That's when the police officer seen us. we tried to outrun the patrol car, lost control, and hit a telephone pole. That's when they caught us with the money and weapons.

These sentences describe all that occurred after the robbery, thus constituting the epilogue. None of these actions would have transpired had not the central issue taken place. The relative proportions of the three sections are distributed as follows:

Task 7

Fill in the blanks.

Prologue: (____% of the narrative) _____ words

Event: (____% of the narrative) _____ words

Epilogue: (____% of the narrative) _____ words

Alternatively, the narrative can be diagrammed as follows:

Task 8

Diagram the allocation of subjective time.

Before:

During:

After:

The analysis of this narrative's formal balance suggests that it approximates a PSTA. Rarely will a narrative balance analysis present an exact one-third, one-third, one-third subjective time allocation. It is those circumstances wherein the balance is significantly disproportional that are of particular interest to the analyst.

Review the account of the robbery once more. Note the absence of the linguistic elements we found in the MacDonald narrative. MacDonald was a physician. The writer of the robbery narrative was not a highly educated person. The presence or absence of these linguistic elements is not a function of education but rather a function of the narrator's goal—to convey or convince.

Task 9

The following two narratives were provided by an individual who was asked to provide one true account and one fictional account. Determine the status of each narrative by determining its form. Remember: the first step in the determination of the form is the location of the beginning of the central issue.

Narrative A

One night I had a visitor. It was a friend or rather a relative. He was from out of town. And he came up for the weekend. When he got to the apartment, I didn't realize anything was wrong. I invited him into my apartment and gave him a mixed drink. Later on he went back to his car and brought out beer that he had been drinking. He also had a gun that he brought into the apartment. He proceeded to get very drunk. I eventually went to sleep. When I woke up he was very drunk and there was beer cans and beer bottles strewn all over my apartment. He was smoking a cigarette and using an ashtray that was full of paper. There was also cigarette butts in my carpeting. I started raising hell and at one time I thought he was going to get violent. He started shaking me and wouldn't let me move. All I could think about was the gun he had brought in. I thought I was going to have to call the police to get rid of him. Finally I just made him drink the end of the beer and I stayed up until he went to sleep. That's it.

Where would you place the beginning of the central issue? In our analysis we can only work with what the narrator has provided. In our endeavor to make sure we keep the analysis process straightforward and avoid over thinking, conceptualize the process in this manner: If I were a police officer responsible for responding to domestic crisis situations, where—according to the narrator—would I come into the picture? It would be at the point at which the narrator declared, "I started raising hell and at one time I thought he was going to get violent." *Raising hell* is a function of anger. Anger is a loss of control, so the situation changes. The central issue is the point when (according to the narrator) the situation changed, whether it is articulated as:

The car went off the side of the bridge; or

And then the next thing I know I heard some screaming, at least my wife; but I thought I heard Kimmie, my older daughter, screaming also; or

When Gene reached the checkout girl, he pulled a pistol out and shouted, "this is a stick-up."

If, in your analysis, you find yourself thinking along the lines of "Well I would have gotten mad when he brought the gun into the house," then you are projecting yourself into the situation. The analysis is not a function of your thought process or how you would react in a similar circumstance. The analysis is being conducted by you based only upon what the teller of the tale has related.

This narrative has a DSTA. Once more, at this point in the analysis process we are not prepared to say that what the narrator asserts is not the truth, as far as it goes. Parenthetically, at this point we are not prepared to say that if it is true then it may not be the whole truth.

Narrative B

> One night when I was sleeping I thought I heard a noise. As I was waking up this hand came down over my mouth and this man started telling me to be still. I tried to scream several times but he sat down on top of me and he kept his hand over my mouth. I guess I kind of went crazy. We started struggling. I bit his hand and I kicked out as hard as I could. He fell off of me and I ran out of the bedroom screaming. he got on top of me again in the living room. I continued screaming. And it must not have been more than two or three minutes altogether but it seemed like a lot longer. Finally one of my neighbors came to the door. And he started pounding on the door and the man got up and ran out the back door. Later on we called the police but they never found the guy. Sometimes it still scares me but I've changed the locks on my apartment. And since then I haven't had anymore trouble. I feel I was lucky that I wasn't raped. That's it.

Where would you place the beginning of the central issue? This central issue starting point in the second narrative may have been a bit easier to determine. The central issue comes into the narrative early on with, "As I was waking up this hand came down over my mouth and this man started telling me to be still." Consequently, Narratives A and B both display a DSTA.

Determining the central issue is not always as easy as we found in Narrative B above. However, even in those narratives where the central issue may be more challenging there is a lifeline.

Task 10

Determine the beginning of the central issue in following narrative.

On Friday ________, 20__ I received a phone call from David Jones, saying he was in Tenn. and wouldn't be in to work the next day. Tried to get someone to cover his schedule and couldn't. Went on about my business. Started paperwork as usual. Check everyone out in their areas. Everything was fine. Finished paperwork. Helped Dan Hartley dump trash, back in locked the back door, and pushed button in on door. Mopped floor behind us, so it wouldn't be streaky. Came up to office, got my stuff together, straightened up. Set the alarm, closed office door and Dan and myself left. We punched out at 24:22 that night. When we got outside, Dan's ride was here, he got in the car and left. Pulled off parking lot about 12:30. Everything was organized and locked up when we left. Came back in about 5:45 am. Everything looked normal. Sandy Jones, Lane Taylor and my wife. We all walked in together. When we got to the door, to go in the back we looked on the hot cook table and there was some glass and a knife. I told the 3 employees not to do anything. I opened the office door and there was the $300 drawer, $950 bag and the deposit bag cut open. Everything was gone. I told the 3 employees to go sit in the dining room and called 911. I told them who I was and what happened. The only thing I touched was the phone. It took approximately 15 min. for the police to arrive. This all took place between 5:45 am and 6:00 am.

Whether in a classroom or online delivery format this narrative always produces a lively discussion with regard to the beginning of the central issue. As a rule, about half the participants will place the beginning of the central issue at "When we got to the door, to go in the back we looked on the hot cook table and there was some glass and a knife." The other half will place the beginning of the central issue at "I opened the office door and there was the $300 drawer, $950 bag and the deposit bag cut open." In either case, you will arrive at the realization that the narrative has a DSTA. To be precise, however, the correct central issue beginning point is the sentence, "When we got to the door, to go in the back we looked on the hot cook table and there was some glass and a knife."

Why? Look at the following sentence. "I told the 3 employees not to do anything." If the glass and the knife were not the tipping point of the narrative he would not have begun issuing orders to "the 3 employees."

As you go forward in your analysis experience you will find when the subjective time allocation is significantly disproportional. Whether you start the central issue at a particular sentence, its preceding sentence, or the following sentence, the finding will still be the same—a disproportional subjective time allocation.

Summary

As we proceed with the process of investigative discourse analysis, the narrative form should be the first focus of analysis. The goal is to determine if the form reflects a balance with regard to the allocation of subjective time or one that may have undergone some degree of manipulation. Whether the manipulation has involved adding to or deleting from the narrative, the action will have affected the narrative form. Once a formal imbalance has caught the analyst's attention, he or he will proceed to the next phase of the analytic process—Semantic Analysis.

Examination

Read the following narrative and answer the questions that follow.

> Uh ... on October the 8th, uh ... Paul Smith had came to my residence uh ... that address there on Route 1, and he asked me to fix uh ... electrical problem that uh ... was occurring his headlight on his car. So uh ... I told him I'd be there in around 10 minutes ... 20 minutes. So I got there, and knocked on his trailer door. Got the key to his automobile and went to proceed to his car to check the headlight and first I went to the front. I pulled the headlights out of the car. Then I went in the car 'cause I seen there was a problem with his headlight. I went in the car and I went under the dash of the car where the electrical wiring and everything, and I started unscrewing the bottom of the dash. Then I pulled out the electrical and I took the relay switch out, which that sits on the top of the left-hand side. So I had to come, what you could say, from the driver side and lay my head on the passenger side to go up here to get another switch wire to relay them to-

gether. And I was laying in the automobile on the floor of the automobile with my legs out the car. And I don't really know what happened on the inside of the house, but Mr. Smith came and the door slammed. At that time I didn't know it was him. I probably thought it was one of the kids or something. And it hit my left ankle and I twisted it with the door. And then being that he seen that the door didn't close all the way slam, he said, "Oh man, I didn't know you was in the car," and that's ... that's basically it right there.

Answer the following questions.

1. The subjective time allocation of this narrative indicates the narrative has a (check one):

_____ Disproportional Subjective Time Allocation

_____ Proportional Subjective Time Allocation

2. The sentence that begins the central issue is: ______________________________

____

____

Read the following narrative and answer the questions that follow.

I was standing in the back storage room talking to Missy Blaylock on the phone. A black man in his late 20's to early thirties came out of the bathroom and handed me a note saying—I have a gun don't do anything stupid or I'll kill you.—I got off the phone with Missy. He showed me the gun (medium pistol). He thought the money was in the candy room and demanded to go in. I took him in there and showed him around. He wanted to know where all the money was and how much there was. I told him. I also told him it would take 10 minutes to open the safe. He said to play it cool and open it while he waited. I set the timer and walked him around the store. After about 5 minutes I walked him back to the front, and took the money out of both end registers. I put the safe money together with it in a blue zipperbag, then put the bag in a small box. I walked him to the back of the store. He left the box on the floor, put the bag up his shirt, then told me to walk him out.

3. The central issue begins with the sentence: ______________________________

____

____

4. The central issues ends with the sentence: ______________________________

____

____

5. This narrative is described as having a (check one):

_____ Disproportional Subjective Time Allocation

_____ Proportional Subjective Time Allocation

6. Explain your rationale for your answer to Question 5. ____________________

____

____

____

Chapter 4

Semantic Analysis of the Narrative

Concepts addressed in this chapter

Lack of conviction about one's own assertions
Use of present tense verbs when describing a past occurrence
Use of more generalized statements
Reduced or eliminated self-references
- non-personal references
- direct references

Non-confirming sentence
Sentences out of sequence
Reduced mean length of utterance
Changes in referencing

Introduction

Now that we have addressed the process for the identification of the narrative form, we can shift our analytic focus to the individual words, phrases, and sentences selectively utilized within a document. As we continue with our examination we will garnet an additional set of terms, concepts, and definitions.

Every word, pause, and hesitation has meaning. The examination of the individual's own words is one of the most fascinating aspects of investigative discourse analysis. It is at this point the analyst seeks to know the *heart* of the speaker by studying the words the teller of the tale provides. At this point, the operative word is *alterity*: the ability to enter into the "world" or another.[1] At this point, the analyst seeks to determine what the person is *really* conveying. Accomplishing that goal in this, the second (Analysis) phase, is critical and linked directly to success in the third (Amplification) phase of the process.

Salient Linguistic Indicators for Analysis

If the individual's word selection is undertaken to misdirect the analyst, an array of semantic indicators can serve to point the way for the planning of the subsequent interview. Because *semantic* refers to word meaning, the analyst can gain a better understanding of what the individual is actually relating if he or she knows for which semantic indicators to search.

1. *Dictionary.com,* http://www.dictionary.com (accessed August 8, 2011).

Keep in mind the three components in investigative discourse analysis:

- what the individual *actually* relates
- what the individual *meant* to relate
- what *determination* the analyst makes regarding the individual's words

The goal of investigative discourse analysis is to align the first and third levels as closely as possible.

❖ Lack of conviction about one's own assertions

This lack of conviction will often be evidenced by modifying or qualifying terms. In chapter one, we examined the MacDonald narrative and the role of modifying terms in the portion of his narrative that dealt with the fight with the people who he reported had invaded his home.

Task 1

The following narrative provides a portion of an account involving missing money. Identify the modifier. What does the application of the modifier in the narrative reveal?

To: Sergeant Webb
From: Katy Brown
Subject: Missing money from Acme Child Center

Following are some of the things I remember about the $212.00 missing from the Acme Child Center.

On Monday, April 28 at sometime between 6:30 and 7:00 a.m., Tom Jones gave me $212.00 in cash to cover tuition of his child. I wrote out a receipt for the money, gave the original to Mr. Jones, attached the pink copy to the cash, and left the yellow copy in the receipt book.

The modifier found therein is "***some of the things** I remember.*" If the narrator is relating "some of the things" she remembers then there are things she remembers that are not included. In the third phase the interviewer will endeavor to determine exactly what those things are which are remembered but not included. The how-to with regard to developing the questions related to these linguistic elements will be addressed in Chapter 6.

❖ Use of present tense verbs when describing a past occurrence

Narrators can, within the body of the narrative, switch from past-tense verbs to present-tense verbs. The narrator will refer to past events as if they were occurring in the present. This transition is known as the *historical present.* The analyst should pay particular attention to those points in the narrative where the speaker shifts to this present tense verb usage. In the Amplification phase, examples of the historical present provide opportunities for amplifying questions.

Task 2

Read the following narrative. Identify the present tense verbs contained therein.

On December 15, 19- in the late afternoon hours, Don L. Harrington, wife Wanda, and friends Amy Barr, Judy Partin and Myself Bob Boone, went to Taylor's to pick up some layaway items. We used two cars because there was some bulky merchandise such as bicycles and a battery-operated car. Don had just gotten his paycheck so instead of making a trip to the bank he would pay the balance of the layaway with his check. Wanda usually handles the finances, so she had Don's check in her purse. So Wanda hands Don his check which in turn he gives it to the layaway clerk. The clerk looked at the check and said that she couldn't accept it but it was obvious that the clerk was inexperienced, because in fact it was the other clerk working in layaway that told the clerk that she would have to check with the manager first. So the clerk takes the check over to the manager and we all see the manager shake her head "no." By this time Don sees that he can't use his check which was a surprise to us because it was a payroll check instead of a personal check. But instead of causing chaos, Don decided to pay for it in cash which Wanda had in her purse. So Don asked her for the money, gave it to the clerk, the clerk gave him the receipt, and we went to the back to pick up the merchandise. In all the confusion, Don thought that Wanda had the check and Wanda thought that Don had it and by this time we had gotten to Don's house. So Don called ABC Company and told the payroll dept. that his check was lost.

Task 3

Review the examples highlighted below.

On December 15, 19- in the late afternoon hours, Don L. Harrington, wife Wanda, and friends Amy Barr, Judy Partin and Myself Bob

Boone, went to Taylor's to pick up some layaway items. We used two cars because there was some bulky merchandise such as bicycles and a battery-operated car. Don had just gotten his paycheck so instead of making a trip to the bank he would pay the balance of the layaway with his check. Wanda usually handles the finances, so she had Don's check in her purse. So Wanda **hands** Don his check which in turn he **gives** it to the layaway clerk. The clerk looked at the check and said that she couldn't accept it but it was obvious that the clerk was inexperienced, because in fact it was the other clerk working in layaway that told the clerk that she would have to check with the manager first. So the clerk **takes** the check over to the manager and we all **see** the manager **shake** her head "no." By this time Don **sees** that he **can't** use his check which was a surprise to us because it was a payroll check instead of a personal check. But instead of causing chaos, Don decided to pay for it in cash which Wanda had in her purse. So Don asked her for the money, gave it to the clerk, the clerk gave him the receipt, and we went to the back to pick up the merchandise. In all the confusion, Don thought that Wanda had the check and Wanda thought that Don had it and by this time we had gotten to Don's house. So Don called ABC Company and told the payroll dept. that his check was lost.

❖ Use of more generalized statements

At some point in the narrative, the individual will relate events, persons, and actions using vague terminology. The analyst may determine that some elements of the narrative are detailed and specific while others are indistinct and undefined.

Task 4

Read the following account of the restaurant break-in once again. In this reading, note where the narrator loses specificity.

On Friday __________, 20__ I received a phone call from David Jones, saying he was in Tenn. and wouldn't be in to work the next day. Tried to get someone to cover his schedule and couldn't. Went on about my business. Started paperwork as usual. Check everyone out in their areas. Everything was fine. Finished paperwork. Helped Dan Hartley dump trash, back in locked the back door, and pushed button in on door. Mopped floor behind us, so it wouldn't be streaky. Came up to office, got my stuff together, straightened up. Set the alarm, closed office door and Dan and myself left. We punched out at 24:22 that night. When we got outside, Dan's ride was here, he got in the car and left. Pulled off parking lot about 12:30. Everything was organized and locked up when we left. Came back in about 5:45 am. Everything looked normal. Sandy Jones, Lane Taylor and my wife. We all walked in together. When we got to the door, to go in the back we looked on the hot cook table and there was some glass and a knife. I told the 3 employees not to do anything. I opened the office door and there was the $300 drawer, $950 bag and the deposit bag cut open. Everything was gone. I told the 3 employees to go sit in the dining room and called 911. I told them who I was and what happened. The only thing I touched was the phone. It took approximately 15 min. for the police to arrive. This all took place between 5:45 am and 6:00 am.

Task 5

Review the highlighted areas:

On Friday —, 19- I received a phone call from David Jones, saying he was in Tenn. and wouldn't be in to work the next day. Tried to get **someone** to cover his schedule and couldn't. Went on about **my business**. **Started paperwork** as usual. **Check everyone** out in their areas. **Everything** was fine. **Finished paperwork**. Helped Dan Hartley

> dump trash, back in locked the back door, and pushed button in on door. Mopped floor behind us, so it wouldn't be streaky. Came up to office, got **my stuff** together, **straightened up**. Set the alarm, closed office door and Dan and myself left. We punched out at 24:22 that night. When we got outside, Dan's ride was here, he got in the car and left. Pulled off parking lot about 12:30. **Everything** was organized and locked up when we left. Came back in about 5:45 am. **Everything** looked normal. Sandy Jones, Lane Taylor and my wife. We all walked in together. When we got to the door, to go in the back we looked on the hot cook table and there was some glass and a knife. I told the 3 employees not to do anything. I opened the office door and there was the $300 drawer, $950 bag and the deposit bag cut open. **Everything** was gone. I told the 3 employees to go sit in the dining room and called 911. I told them who I was and what happened. The only thing I touched was the phone. It took approximately 15 min. for the police to arrive. This all took place between 5:45 am and 6:00 am.

The analyst would expect to find instances of explicit detail in the narrative, including information not essential to the flow of the narrative. Referencing back to Aristotle, *whole* narratives will tend to be specific and give details consistently throughout the narrative because the goal of the narrator is to convey information readily rather than to endeavor to convince.

Task 6

Once more, read the narrative of the armed robbery. Note the specificity provided throughout the narrative.

> On the day of August 17, 19__, I with Gene Smith drove to a grocery store and parked outside in the parking lot. We sat for 20 minutes watching the store. When there was no more than 2 customers in there me and Gene left the car and went into the store. After we were in the store I went toward the back of the store while Gene got in the checkout line. When Gene reached the checkout girl, he pulled

> a pistol out and shouted, "this is a stick-up." This was my signal to come back up front. Upon getting there Gene told the checkout girl to open the cash register. After she had it open, I grabbed a paper bag and stuffed the money into the bag. Before leaving the store, I locked the cashier and the meat market man into the freezer. We left the store, got into a green truck, fled down Main Street, made a wrong turn on a one-way street. That's when the police officer seen us. We tried to outrun the patrol car, lost control, and hit a telephone pole. That is when they caught us with the money and weapons.

From this brief portion of the narrative, we know as the following details:

- the specific date
- the name of the other individual involved
- the robbery site
- the length of time spent in the parking lot before the robbery
- the number of customers in the store
- where both the individual and his accomplice went upon entering the store
- the color of the truck
- the name of the street down which they fled
- exactly what the truck hit
- what they had when the police caught them.

Task 7

Read the following portion of a narrative related to a homicide. Note the locations where specific details are provided. At other points, however, temporal lacunae and generalized statements have replaced the specificity. As always, the analyst searches for *change* in linguistic behavior.

> Jack Jones came in about 1:00 p.m. or a little after. Then he said come here I want to ask you something I said what. He didn't want people to know about him getting tickets to leisure living show. And asked me how many I wanted. I said 2 or 3 if I could get them. He said let me call his wife—Marie—he had another beer talk to Ronnie and Ted a minute then said he was going to find out how many she

> wanted had 2 more beers left and said I will be back later with the tickets that was about 2:00 p.m. Then Lea came in and I was taping a movie on the big t.v. The rest of the people were watching the movie and the ball game. She said put that big t.v. on the ball game. I said Lea I got the game on the other t.v. I got 15 minutes before this movie go's off then I will turn it, she got mad and left. Then Lanny Hinkle came in, Bob, Larry, Duke. And I got real busy, people just kept coming in. Janie came in at 3:30 p.m. Then at 6:00 I rung out and she counted the money behind me. I then walked around and wiped down the counter and ash trays. Some people talked to me asking how was I doing and how was Billy doing. Then at 7:00 I had my first beer. Sat down with Bonnie and Mitch watched some people shoot pool. Then about 9:00 Lucie called crying and she said her D.R. had words and left her would I please come and get her at the Winner Circle. I said yes.

The first portion of this narrative includes many details: who came in and at what time, what the discussion was about, names, relationships, and problems with customers and the television. Then we see a rapid leap of time, from 3:30 to 6:00. Two and a half hours have passed instantly, and we have learned nothing of what occurred during that time. Reading along very quickly, it is 7:00 and then 9:00. The narrator has covered six hours from 3:00 to 9:00 with a minimum amount of vague, subjective time.

Once more in the MacDonald narrative, there is a striking lack of specificity in his account of fighting for his life with the individuals who he claimed had attacked him and killed his pregnant wife and two daughters.

> And then the next thing I know I heard **some screaming**, at least my wife; but I thought I heard Kimmie, my older daughter, screaming also. And I sat up. The kitchen light was on, and I saw **some people** at the foot of the bed. So, I don't know if I really said anything or I was getting ready to say something. **This** happened real fast. You know, when you talk about **it**, **it** sounds like **it** took forever; but **it** didn't take

forever. And so, I sat up; and at first I thought it was—I just could see three people, and I don't know if I—If I heard **the girl** first—or I think I saw her first. I think two of **the men** separated sort of at the end of my couch, and I keep—all I saw was **some people** really. And **this guy** started talking down between the coffee table and the couch, and he raised **something** over his head and just sort of then—sort of all together—I just got a glance of **this girl** with kind of a light on her face.

❖ Reduced or eliminated self-references.

This avoidance of self-referencing by the narrator is disclosed in sentences beginning with verbs or in descriptions of activities in which the narrator was a participant, but which include no references to his involvement, as in the following example.

Went to work I think about 8:00. Worked to about 7:30. Stopped gas station in Townsboro got some gas. Went to my brother's house took a shower. Went to my brother Scott Weaver's house in Turnville. Stayed about an hour. Left there went through Fremont saw a friend Peggy going in her house. Talked to her for few minutes. Stopped at my mother's house. Went in for a few minutes. Came back out got in car was going to my brother's house who I live with now. Smelt something burning thought it was ash tray. But it was not. Got to looking around saw smoke coming out around heater vent controls. Pulled over looked to see what was going on it was just smoking around dash. I did not see any fire. Got scared ran to my mother's house. She called fire department. When we got back it was on fire.

Task 8

In the next example, note the point at which self-reference (i.e., the pronoun *I*) disappears and then reappears within the narrative from the narrative.

On July 18th, 1969, at approximately 11:15 P.M. in Chappaquiddick, Martha's Vineyard, Massachusetts, I was driving my car on Main

> Street on my way to get the ferry back to Edgartown. I was unfamiliar with the road and turned right onto Dike Road, instead of bearing hard left on Main Street. After proceeding for approximately one-half mile on Dike Road I descended a hill and came upon a narrow bridge.
>
> The car went off the side of the bridge. There was one passenger with me, one Miss _______, a former secretary of my brother Sen. Robert Kennedy. The car turned over and sank into the water and landed with the roof resting on the bottom.
>
> I attempted to open the door and the window of the car but have no recollection of how I got out of the car. I came to the surface and then repeatedly dove down to the car in an attempt to see if the passenger was still in the car. I was unsuccessful in the attempt. I recall walking back to where my friends were eating. There was a car parked in front of the cottage and I climbed into the backseat. I then asked for someone to bring me back to Edgartown. I remember walking around for a period then going back to my hotel room. When I fully realized what had happened this morning, I immediately contacted the police.

The pronoun *I* is used 13 times within the narrative. It occurs at 3 points in the prologue of the narrative. The pronoun *I* is not used at all during the description of the narrative's central issue. Instead, the writer transitions from the use of the pronoun *I* (active voice) to "The car went off the side of the bridge" (passive voice). The individual could have written, "I drove off the bridge," or "we turned over and sank," but he did not; it was "the car" that did so. During the epilogue of the narrative, the first-person pronoun reappears and is used 10 times. By tracking the pronoun *I*, we can learn much about the events and actions related by the speaker in conjunction with the pronoun's ebb and flow throughout the narrative.

Sentences such as "The car went off the side of the bridge," and "The car turned over and sank into the water and landed with the roof resting on the bottom," are *non-personal references.* A non-personal reference is a sentence in which the speaker is not present in the sentence. As we illustrate the concept to the participants in our classes, there is no one home in the sentence.

Another way in which the presenter may avoid self-referencing is through the use of *direct referencing*. With direct referencing, the individual will begin to make reference to himself using the pronoun *you*. Examples of direct referencing found in the MacDonald narrative include:

- "when you talk about it, it sounds like it took forever"
- "you start getting chills"
- "you weren't really that bad, but that's what happens when you get a pneumothorax. You—you think you can't breathe"

Direct references can also be displayed as *you know*. This phrasing can be an effort on the part of the speaker to be certain the listener is accepting what has been asserted. Pay attention to clustering of *you know* and note the topic on the table at the point the clustering manifests.

Locations in the word selection, where non-personal or direct references are used provide meaningful opportunities for the development of amplifying questions during the third phase.

❖ Non-confirming sentence

In a non-confirming sentence, the presenter endeavors to indicate that an action took place without specifically stating the action *did* occur. Terms such as *tried, attempted, started* and using the infinitive of a verb (for example, to start) are methodologies undertaken to give the impression that an action took place or occurred. Additionally, a non-confirming sentence can be constructed to infer that an action took place, leaving it to the reader (or listener, as the case may be) to make the inference. Let's look at some examples.

In the narrative involving the accident with the car going off of the side of the bridge, the writer states, "I then asked for someone to bring me back to Edgartown." The inference the writer wants the reader to make is that someone *did* take him back to Edgartown, which was not the case. In a later statement the writer revealed that he swam back to Edgartown.

In the narrative below involving an encounter at a party, we note the high usage of the term *started.*

> I had been at a party for approx. 3 hours when I had to go to the bathroom. As I was walking to the bathroom I **started** talking to this girl because we had to wait in line. She was looking a little drunk but so was I. She went into the bathroom and when she opened the door to exit I quickly ran past her in a hurry to use the bathroom. As I was using the toilet I noticed that she was still in there. When I was finished she **started** to rub my chest. I then ask her her name and she told me. We **started** to kiss and she fell onto the bathroom floor. We continued to kiss then she **started** rubbing my crotch. So I began to do the same to her. I continued to rub her then I inserted my middle finger into her vagina. She said she was a virgin so I didn't continue for too long. By that time people were banging on the door so I got off the floor. She then **started** to suck my penis but only for a few sec-

> onds. I then helped her up off the floor. We straightened up our clothes and then proceeded to exit the bathroom. When we left the bathroom some of my friends and other people were outside the door waiting to use the bathroom. I walked up the steps and she sat down on the steps and was talking to another guy. (Davy Jones?) I left the party shortly afterwards and was gone for about 30 minutes. When I got back all the people were asking me what happened. I didn't even know what they were talking about until someone said this girl claims I raped her. I then was approached by 2 guys that I didn't know. They asked me if I had been with this girl and I said "yes we messed around in the bathroom." I **started** to walk away when he hit me on the top of my head. Then a large fight broke out. The police arrived and it was over.

The salient point for the analyst in the preceding narrative is that the narrator indicates that actions "started" to happen—not that the action *did* happen. As an illustration in our classes, we use the sentence, "I started to pay you the money that I owe to you." As we think this sentence through we understand exactly who, after all is said and done, still has the money. I did not pay you the money, I only *started* to. Another illustration is, "I started to give my Harley to you." But who still has the Harley?

In the narrative involving the vehicle fire, we note a high usage of the word *attempt.*

> On 21 September approximately 1730 hrs myself and William Turner were on our way to Camp McCall to retrieve personal items. At the junction of Chicken Rd and Plank Rd the vehicle ceased running. An **attempt** was made to start the vehicle. It was, however, unsuccessful. Due to a prior obligation I opted to leave the vehicle on the side of the Rd. The MP's were contacted in this regard. At 12 noon 22 Sept I returned to the vehicle to inspect it and retrieve my wallet. At 1630 that same day I returned with Mr. Turner in his vehicle to **attempt** to diagnose the problem and repair it, leaving a tow

> truck an open option. I **attempted** to start the vehicle. It ran for approximately 30 seconds. I noticed the digital dash displaying strange numbers i.e. 35 mph and the car was standing still. After the car stalled I raised the hood to check the electric fuel pump pressure. I, therefore, left the key in the on position. As I checked it from outside the vehicle I noticed smoke rising from the passenger side compartment. I opened the door to investigate and at that time under the dash I saw smoke and small flames. I **attempted** to extinguish the flames with my hands. At that time SGT Gary Regan 1/504 showed up at the scene. He also **attempted.** I ran to Mr. Turner's vehicle to see if he had water. He had a rag. I ran back and **attempted** to put it out, but the fire was unable to be brought under control. At this time I flagged down a vehicle to contact the authorities. The man in the vehicle agreed to do so. I continued to control traffic until the authorities arrived.

In the above narrative we observe the narrator *attempted* to do a goodly number of actions. *Attempting* is not *doing*. Going back to our previous classroom examples with related modifications, "I attempted to pay you the money that I owe to you," and "I attempted to give my Harley to you." Who is still sitting on the Harley with the money in his pocket?

Let us review the account once more focusing on the examples of non-confirming sentencing using the infinitive form of verbs:

> On 21 September Approximately 1730 hrs myself and William Turner were on our way to Camp McCall **to retrieve** personal items. At the junction of Chicken Rd and Plank Rd the vehicle ceased running. An attempt was made **to start** the vehicle. It was, however, unsuccessful. Due to a prior obligation I opted **to leave** the vehicle on the side of the Rd. The MP's were contacted in this regard. At 12 noon 22 Sept I returned to the vehicle **to inspect** it and retrieve my wallet. At 1630 that same day I returned with Mr. Turner in his vehicle

to attempt to diagnose the problem and repair it, leaving a tow truck an open option. I attempted **to start** the vehicle. It ran for approximately 30 seconds. I noticed the digital dash displaying strange numbers i.e. 35 mph and the car was standing still. After the car stalled I raised the hood **to check** the electric fuel pump pressure. I, therefore, left the key in the on position. As I checked it from outside the vehicle I noticed smoke rising from the passenger side compartment. I opened the door **to investigate** and at that time under the dash I saw smoke and small flames. I attempted **to extinguish** the flames with my hands. At that time SGT Gary Regan 1/504 showed up at the scene. He also attempted. I ran to Mr. Turner's vehicle **to see** if he had water. He had a rag. I ran back and attempted to put it out, but the fire was unable to be brought under control. At this time I flagged down a vehicle to contact the authorities. The man in the vehicle agreed to do so. I continued to control traffic until the authorities arrived.

Task 9

Can you find some examples of verb infinitives in the above that were not highlighted?

Answer: ______________________________

____

____

In the examination of the verb infinitives within a narrative, the analyst should mentally add the phrase *I was going* in front of the infinitive to gain a perspective of what the narrator is endeavoring to assert. For example:

- *I was going* to investigate is not *I investigated;*
- *I was going* to extinguish is not *I extinguished;*
- *I was going* to see if he had water is not *I went to see if he had water.*

Now, going back to our previous examples with the related non-confirming modifications, "I *was going* to pay you the money that I owe to you," and "I *was going* to give my Harley to you." Who is still riding with the money to spend?

Task 10

The following narrative was produced by a nurse who was working on a hospital wing during the time when two fires occurred. After she was presented with the results of a formal analysis of her narrative in the amplification phase, she confessed to starting the fires. Find the examples of non-confirming sentences within the account

> I arrived for work about 0640. After listening to report and assessed my patients in 5016, 5039, 5041. This was finished by approximately 0830. I started on passing 0900 medications with various interruptions—i.e.: salvaging an I.V. in 5041 and filling the feeding bag in 5016. I cannot honestly give any times for these activities. I believe the first fire was between 0930-1000. I know I did need to retrieve my inhaler from my car since I have asthma that is triggered by smoke. After recovering from that event I continued my rounds on patients and took report from Joan to enable her to go to lunch. During this time, the secretary Linda and D.A. told me about some threatening phone calls while I was in the nurse's station trying to do some charting. After Joan came back from lunch she asked all of us (nurses, secretary and assistants) to be more aware of any unusual people or situations. Shortly after this, I started to have another asthma attack and told Joan. The alarms then went off and the fire doors closed. As we went down the hall to close doors, someone opened 5019 and the smoke came out. I left as quickly as I could and sat outside until I could recover enough to function. The remaining 2 hours were spent trying to finish my workload and hoping nothing else would happen. Also, about 11:15 I did an admission on 5014 but this did not take up more than 20 minutes.

❖ Sentences out of sequence

Previously we have addressed the flow of the narrative. Ideally the narrative will proceed from the beginning—starting point—until the end. The analyst should always note sentences that are out of order with the flow of the narrative. In some instances, the narrator will step away from the narrative, make a comment and step back into the narrative. As a result, the flow of the narrative is disrupted. In general conversation this dynamic is known as an *aside.* In the narrator's mind there is a connection with the main topic of the narrative. It remains for the analyst to make the connection.

In other instances the narrator will backtrack and provide a sentence containing information that should have been presented earlier in the narrative. For example: "After the car stalled I raised the hood to check the electric fuel pump pressure. I, therefore, left the key in the on position."

Often sentences out of sequence contain some of the most revealing information and provide significant opportunities for developing questions in the third amplifying phase of the process. In the MacDonald narrative, examples of sentences out of sequence include:

- "See, I work out with the boxing gloves sometimes. I was then."
- "That's one of the symptoms of shock; you start getting chills."
- "Now, I remember I saw—I don't know if it was the first or second trip into the bedroom to see my wife—but I saw the back door was open, but that's immaterial, I guess."

At the end of the narrative related to the fires in the hospital, we see the narrator also ended the narrative with a sentence out of sequence: "Also, about 11:15 I did an admission on 5014 but this did not take up more than 20 minutes."

Task 11

Find the out-of-sequence sentences in the following narrative.

After leaving the building after work, at approximately 1:00 a.m. on 1/10/__ I stopped at a Quick Pick Store to get a pack of cigarettes. Store at Smith and Tucker. While doing so a silver '88 or '89 Toyota Celica (I believe) pulled in up to pay phone area where I was. A white male, age late twenties/early thirties, 5'10', 190 lbs with a yellow tie, broad shoulders, muscular build, thick neck, got out of car, went to phone, put money in, dialed # and started talking. I finished throwing the wrapper from my cigarettes away and turned to walk to the car when the man grabbed me from behind and began choking me and pushing me toward his car telling me to get in or he would kill me. When I was able to get a breath, I started screaming, and he pushed me into my car. I began blowing the horn. At one point I asked if he was a coach or with a football team in town. He said yes then quickly said no — not to worry about where he was from. He said he was drunk and smelled that way. I would say he was definitely intoxicated. He proceeded to fight with me, choking me, twisting my arm (right) behind my back and said quote 'I'm drunk, my dick is hard and I'm going to fuck you'—unquote. His intent was more than clear. Finally after my loud protests and physical disapproval, he got in his car and backed out with the lights off. I didn't see license plate. He also asked where he could find some pussy in town. Therefore, I believe him to be from out-of-town. He was also wearing a college ring on his left ring finger.

❖ Reduced mean length of utterance (MLU)

The mean length of utterance consists of the average number of words in a sentence found within the narrative. To calculate the MLU:

1. Number the sentences found within the narrative.
2. Count and record the number of words in each sentence in the narrative.
3. Total the number of words in all of the sentences for a total narrative word count.
4. Divide the total narrative word count by the number of sentences to obtain the MLU for the narrative.
5. Identify those sentences that are below the MLU.

The formula for this process can be written as:

MLU = *Number of Words* divided by *Number of Sentences or*

$$\text{MLU} = \frac{\textit{Number of Words}}{\textit{Number of Sentences}}$$

Let's walk our way through the process.

Step One

Read the following narrative.

On 21 September approximately 1730 hrs myself and William Turner were on our way to Camp McCall to retrieve personal items. At the junction of Chicken Rd and Plank Rd the vehicle ceased running. An attempt was made to start the vehicle. It was, however, unsuccessful. Due to a prior obligation I opted to leave the vehicle on the side of the Rd. The MP's were contacted in this regard. At 12 noon 22 Sept

I returned to the vehicle to inspect it and retrieve my wallet. At 1630 that same day I returned with Mr. Turner in his vehicle to attempt to diagnose the problem and repair it, leaving a tow truck an open option. I attempted to start the vehicle. It ran for approximately 30 seconds. I noticed the digital dash displaying strange numbers i.e. 35 mph and the car was standing still. After the car stalled I raised the hood to check the electric fuel pump pressure. I, therefore, left the key in the on position. As I checked it from outside the vehicle I noticed smoke rising from the passenger side compartment. I opened the door to investigate and at that time under the dash I saw smoke and small flames. I attempted to extinguish the flames with my hands. At that time SGT Gary Regan 1/504 showed up at the scene. He also attempted. I ran to Mr. Turner's vehicle to see if he had water. He had a rag. I ran back and attempted to put it out, but the fire was unable to be brought under control. At this time I flagged down a vehicle to contact the authorities. The man in the vehicle agreed to do so. I continued to control traffic until the authorities arrived.

Step Two

- Number the sentences found within the narrative. There are 24 sentences in the narrative. On a separate sheet of paper, number 1 to 24 down the left-hand side of the paper. Lined paper works best. At the top of the sheet, label this worksheet "Vehicle Fire Number 3" and hold onto the sheet. We will be returning to this sheet as we progress in the analysis process.
- Count and record the number of words in each sentence in the narrative. Your sheet should look something like the following:

Narrative Analysis Outline

Sentence	
1.	21 words
2.	13 words
3.	8 words
4.	4 words
5.	17 words

6. 7 words
7. 17 words
8. 29 words
9. 6 words
10. 6 words
11. 17 words
12. 15 words
13. 9 words
14. 17 words
15. 19 words
16. 9 words
17. 12 words
18. 3 words
19. 12 words
20. 4 words
21. 19 words
22. 12 words
23. 9 words
24. 9 words

Step Three

- Add the number of words in all of the sentences for a total narrative word count. Your count should be 294 words. The writer used 294 words to relate what occurred with regard to the vehicle fire.

Step Four

- Divide the total narrative word count by the number of sentences to obtain the narrative MLU. Two hundred, ninety-four (294) words divided by 24 sentences equals 12.25. By rounding down we arrive at an MLU of 12.

Step Five

- Identify those sentences that are less than the MLU.

Answer: ____

____

____

Narrative Analysis Outline

Sentence

1. 21 words
2. 13 words
3. 8 words*

4. 4 words*
5. 17 words
6. 7 words*
7. 17 words
8. 29 words
9. 6 words*
10. 6 words*
11. 17 words
12. 15 words
13. 9 words*
14. 17 words
15. 19 words
16. 9 words*
17. 12 words
18. 3 words*
19. 12 words
20. 4 words*
21. 19 words
22. 12 words
23. 9 words*
24. 9 words*

❖ Changes in referencing

Two important analysis requisites regarding references are:

- trace the references for the topic of the narrative throughout the narrative
- note any change of referencing for a given item

Nothing happens in a vacuum. There is always cause and effect. *Talking* does not equal *speaking.* Both are verbs indicating communication but they are not the same. *Bill* does not equal *my partner.* They both are references to the same person but the relationship is different. Term *apple* equals term *apple.* Term *apple* does not equal term *orange.*

Task 12

Read the following narrative relating to the vehicle fire again. In this reading, locate changes in referencing for the writer's mode of transportation, an individual and a group. You will find it helpful and enlightening to list the words by the appropriate sentence in the exercise above.

Answer: ____

____

____

On 21 September Approximately 1730 hrs myself and William

Turner were on our way to Camp McCall to retrieve personal items. At the junction of Chicken Rd and Plank Rd the vehicle ceased running. An attempt was made to start the vehicle. It was, however, unsuccessful. Due to a prior obligation I opted to leave the vehicle on the side of the Rd. The MP's were contacted in this regard. At 12 noon 22 Sept I returned to the vehicle to inspect it and retrieve my wallet. At 1630 that same day I returned with Mr. Turner in his vehicle to attempt to diagnose the problem and repair it, leaving a tow truck an open option. I attempted to start the vehicle. It ran for approximately 30 seconds. I noticed the digital dash displaying strange numbers i.e. 35 mph and the car was standing still. After the car stalled I raised the hood to check the electric fuel pump pressure. I, therefore, left the key in the on position. As I checked it from outside the vehicle I noticed smoke rising from the passenger side compartment. I opened the door to investigate and at that time under the dash I saw smoke and small flames. I attempted to extinguish the flames with my hands. At that time SGT Gary Regan 1/504 showed up at the scene. He also attempted. I ran to Mr. Turner's vehicle to see if he had water. He had a rag. I ran back and attempted to put it out, but the fire was unable to be brought under control. At this time I flagged down a vehicle to contact the authorities. The man in the vehicle agreed to do so. I continued to control traffic until the authorities arrived.

Task 13

Return to the MacDonald narrative in Chapter 1. Find the terms that MacDonald used for the attackers and his family. Term *apple* equals term *apple*.

Answer: ______________________________

____

____

____

Task 14

Read the following narrative. Find the writer's reference for what was stolen. Trace the use of the term backward to the beginning of the narrative. Because term *alpha* equals term *alpha,* what was the reference when the term was used? What other change in referencing can you find?

Answer: ____

____

____

On Friday __________, 20__ I received a phone call from David Jones, saying he was in Tenn. and wouldn't be in to work the next day. Tried to get someone to cover his schedule and couldn't. Went on about my business. Started paperwork as usual. Check everyone out in their areas. Everything was fine. Finished paperwork. Helped Dan Hartley dump trash, back in locked the back door, and pushed button in on door. Mopped floor behind us, so it wouldn't be streaky. Came up to office, got my stuff together, straightened up. Set the alarm, closed office door and Dan and myself left. We punched out at 24:22 that night. When we got outside, Dan's ride was here, he got in the car and left. Pulled off parking lot about 12:30. Everything was organized and locked up when we left. Came back in about 5:45am. Everything looked normal. Sandy Jones, Lane Taylor and my wife. We all walked in together. When we got to the door, to go in the back we looked on the hot cook table and there was some glass and a knife. I told the 3 employees not to do anything. I opened the office door and there was the $300 drawer, $950 bag and the deposit bag cut open. Everything was gone. I told the 3 employees to go sit in the dining room and called 911. I told them who I was and what happened. The only thing I touched was the phone. It took approximately 15 min. for the police to arrive. This all took place between 5:45 am and 6:00 am.

A Semantic Analysis Walk-through

Based on what we have addressed regarding semantic analysis, we will now collaboratively disassemble and analyze a narrative, sentence by sentence. As we progress we will pose questions and provide the opportunity to fill in the blanks. This exercise is designed to give you insight as to how the analyst should be questioning and thinking. Our goal is to figuratively step back just a bit and let you lead the way. We will examine the sentences in detail to determine what the individual has revealed to us.

Task 15

Read the following narrative once more. Then read the narrative still again. During the second reading you may find it helpful to enhance the learning process if you identify and label the investigative discourse analysis elements we have addressed to this point. Some analysts have found it helpful to use highlighters—one color for verbs, another color for nouns, etc.

> One night I had a visitor. It was a friend or rather a relative. He was from out of town. And he came up for the weekend. When he got to the apartment, I didn't realize anything was wrong. I invited him into my apartment and gave him a mixed drink. Later on he went back to his car and brought out beer that he had been drinking. He also had a gun that he brought into the apartment. He proceeded to get very drunk. I eventually went to sleep. When I woke up he was very drunk and there was beer cans and beer bottles strewn all over my apartment. He was smoking a cigarette and using an ashtray that was full of paper. There was also cigarette butts in my carpeting. I started raising hell and at one time I thought he was going to get violent. He started shaking me and wouldn't let me move. All I could think about was the gun he had brought in. I thought I was going to have to call the police to get rid of him. Finally I just made him drink the end of the beer and I stayed up until he went to sleep. That's it.

1. There are __________ sentences in the narrative. In the narrative the total word count is _______. The MLU for this narrative is _______. The sentences with fewer words than the MLU are: ____?

One night I had a visitor.

2. There are ____ words in this sentence. This sentence lacks specificity. The analyst would ask, "What night?" and "Who was the visitor?"

It was a friend or rather a relative.

3. There are ____ words in this sentence.

He was from out of town.

4. Where was he from? There are ____ words in this sentence.

And he came up for the weekend.

5. What is meant by *up*? ________________________ There are ____ words in this setence.

When he got to the apartment, I didn't realize anything was wrong.

6. This is an example of ______________. We learn that at some later point the individual did realize something was wrong. What was wrong? __________________________ If we cannot tell what was wrong from the narrative itself, we are open to the possibility that some information is missing. There are ____ words in this sentence.

I invited him into my apartment and gave him a mixed drink.

7. Pay attention to "invited," "my," and "gave." There are ____ words in this sentence.

Later on he went back to his car and brought out beer that he had been drinking.

8. "Later" is an indication of a ________________________________. Between the drink in the previous sentence and the beginning of this sentence, some unit of narrative has been deleted. What? ____________________________ There are ____ words in this sentence.

He also had a gun that he brought into the apartment.

9. There are ____ words in this sentence. Notice how "my" apartment has become "the" apartment. What was the antecedent to this change? __________________________________ "My" is an example of ____________________________.

He proceeded to get very drunk.

10. Note the adverb *very*. What does it's usage indicate? __________________________ There are ____ words in this sentence.

I eventually went to sleep.

11. Another ________________________ occurs with "eventually." Something is missing. What is it? ______________________________________ What is meant by "sleep?" Is to go to "sleep" the same as to go to "bed?" __________ There are ____ words in this sentence.

When I woke up he was very drunk and there was beer cans and beer bottles strewn all over my apartment.

12. Another ____________________________occurs, and "the" apartment has once again become "my" apartment. What was the antecedent to this change? ___________________ There are ____ words in this sentence.

He was smoking a cigarette and using an ashtray that was full of paper.

13. There are ____ words in this sentence.

There was also cigarette butts in my carpeting.

14. Note the use of the possessive pronoun "my." The linguistic terms for *my* is ____________. There are ____ words in this sentence.

I started raising hell and at one time I thought he was going to get violent.

15. What is meant by "started raising hell?" _____________________________________ "Thought" is an example of a _________________________. When was the specific "time?"____________________ What is meant by "violent?" ____________________ There are ____ words in this sentence.

He started shaking me and wouldn't let me move.

16. There are ____ words in this sentence.

All I could think about was the gun he had brought in.

17. There are ____ words in this sentence.

I thought I was going to have to call the police to get rid of him.

18. There are ____ words in this sentence.

Finally I just made him drink the end of the beer and I stayed up until he went to sleep.

19. "Finally" is another indication of a ____________________. Note the words *just made.* Does logic or even common sense suggest that a man who is drunk, violent, and armed with a gun can be "made" to do much of anything? _______ There are ____ words in this sentence.

Now let us take the opportunity to transition the analysis process to the next level.

What follows is the account of the vehicle fire with the sentences numbered. Read the account once more.

1. On 21 September Approximately 1730 hrs myself and William Turner were on our way to Camp McCall to retrieve personal items.
2. At the junction of Chicken Rd and Plank Rd the vehicle ceased running.
3. An attempt was made to start the vehicle.
4. It was, however, unsuccessful.
5. Due to a prior obligation I opted to leave the vehicle on the side of the Rd.
6. The MP's were contacted in this regard.
7. At 12 noon 22 Sept I returned to the vehicle to inspect it and retrieve my wallet.
8. At 1630 that same day I returned with Mr. Turner in his vehicle to attempt to diagnose the problem and repair it, leaving a tow truck an open option.
9. I attempted to start the vehicle.
10. It ran for approximately 30 seconds.
11. I noticed the digital dash displaying strange numbers i.e. 35 mph and the car was standing still.
12. After the car stalled I raised the hood to check the electric fuel pump pressure.
13. I, therefore, left the key in the on position.
14. As I checked it from outside the vehicle I noticed smoke rising from the passenger side compartment.
15. I opened the door to investigate and at that time under the dash I saw smoke and small flames.
16. I attempted to extinguish the flames with my hands.
17. At that time SGT Gary Regan 1/504 showed up at the scene.
18. He also attempted.
19. I ran to Mr. Turner's vehicle to see if he had water.
20. He had a rag.

21. I ran back and attempted to put it out, but the fire was unable to be brought under control.
22. At this time I flagged down a vehicle to contact the authorities.
23. The man in the vehicle agreed to do so.
24. I continued to control traffic until the authorities arrived.

Task 16

The terms for the linguistic components found in the sentences are listed by the sentence numbers below. However, it will be your charge to attach the words with the components. Specifically, if there is a marker word listed, name the marker word in the sentence. Additionally, what linguistic components found in any sentences have not been listed?

Narrative Analysis Outline

Sentence 1. 21 words marker word, non-confirming, generalized term

Answer: ____

____

____

Sentence 2. 13 words temporal lacuna, non-personal reference

Answer: ____

____

____

Sentence 3. 8 words* non-confirming, non-confirming

Answer: ____

____

____

Sentence 4. 4 words* non-personal reference

Answer: ____

____

____

Sentence 5. 17 words generalized term

Answer: ____

____

Sentence 6. 7 words* Non-personal reference, generalized term

Answer: ______________________________

____

____

Sentence 7. 17 words temporal lacuna, non-confirming

Answer: ______________________________

____

____

Sentence 8. 29 words temporal lacuna, non-confirming, non-confirming

Answer: ______________________________

____

____

Sentence 9. 6 words* non-confirming

Answer: ______________________________

____

____

Sentence 10. 6 words* non-personal reference

Answer: ______________________________

____

____

Sentence 11. 17 words

Answer: ______________________________

____

____

Sentence 12. 15 words temporal lacuna, non-confirming

Answer: ______________________________

____

____

Sentence 13. 9 words* sentence out of sequence

Answer: ______________________________

____

____

Sentence 14. 17 words temporal lacuna

Answer: ______________________________

____

____

Sentence 15. 19 words non-confirming

Answer: ______________________________

____

____

Sentence 16. 9 words* non-confirming, non-confirming

Answer: ______________________________

____

____

Sentence 17. 12 words temporal lacuna

Answer: ______________________________

____

____

Sentence 18. 3 words* non-confirming

Answer: ______________________________

____

____

Sentence 19. 12 words non-confirming

Answer: ______________________________

____

____

Sentence 20. 4 words*

Answer: ______________________________

____

____

Sentence 21. 19 words non-confirming, abjuration term, non-confirming

Answer: ______________________________

____

____

Sentence 22. 12 words temporal lacuna

Answer: ______________________________

____

____

Sentence 23. 9 words*

Answer: ______________________________

____

____

Sentence 24. 9 words*

Answer: ______________________________

____

____

The central issue in the above narrative began with sentence number _______.

The central issue in the above narrative ended with sentence number _______.

Describe the subjective time allocation of the narrative:

Answer: ______________________________

____

____

Task 17

Using the terms, concepts, definitions, and process addressed to this point, conduct an analysis of the following narrative as completely as you can.

> On Friday __________, 20__ I received a phone call from David Jones, saying he was in Tenn. and wouldn't be in to work the next day. Tried to get someone to cover his schedule and couldn't. Went on about my business. Started paperwork as usual. Check everyone out in their areas. Everything was fine. Finished paperwork. Helped Dan Hartley dump trash, back in locked the back door, and pushed button in on door. Mopped floor behind us, so it wouldn't be streaky. Came up to office, got my stuff together, straightened up. Set the alarm, closed office door and Dan and myself left. We punched out at 24:22 that night. When we got outside, Dan's ride was here, he got in the car and left. Pulled off parking lot about 12:30. Everything was organized and locked up when we left. Came back in about 5:45 am. Everything looked normal. Sandy Jones, Lane Taylor and my wife. We all walked in together. When we got to the door, to go in the back we looked on the hot cook table and there was some glass and a knife. I told the 3 employees not to do anything. I opened the office door and there was the $300 drawer, $950 bag and the deposit bag cut open. Everything was gone. I told the 3 employees to go sit in the dining room and called 911. I told them who I was and what happened. The only thing I touched was the phone. It took approximately 15 min. for the police to arrive. This all took place between 5:45 am and 6:00 am.

Not every narrative or verbatim document will lend itself to the word count and determination of the mean length of utterance. The depth of an analysis is always going to be a judgment call on the part of the analyst based on the totality of the circumstance. The following will provide the opportunity to undertake a semantic-only analysis.

Task 18

Conduct an analysis of the next narrative and answer the questions that follow it. In this exercise, you do not have to determine the sentence count, word count, or the MLU. This is an unusually long narrative. Additionally, as the narrative addresses a number of days, the balance or form of the narrative will not be addressed in this exercise. That being the case, this lengthy narrative will provide an opportunity to examine the linguistic analysis components we have addressed to this point. Do not hesitate to mark the component as you progress.

Friday 9/20 noon

Went to lunch with Don Robbinson and Scott Smithfield (company staff). Ate at Dick's Last Resort (West End). Returned to office approximately at 1:00. University of North Texas students were visiting office and gave short demonstration on computer techniques. Also talked with Marvin Finks (Partner) regarding audit proposal for Hartly Transportation. Left office at 4:30-4:45 with Lon Berkowitz (Audit Manager). He and I went to Late Night (West End) and split a pitcher of beer and played 3 games of pool. Left at 5:30. Arrived home at 5:50. Changed clothes and walked the dog. Walk was down Paulus around YMCA back up Tremont and home. Walk was approximately 15-20 minutes. Turned on TV and went through mail. Mandie arrived home at 6:30. She went to bedroom and wrapped my birthday gift (a tie purchased that day at Macy's). I opened gift and read card. Nephews (Bernard and Frankie Morgonton) brought up crayon drawings they had done wishing me a happy birthday. They went back downstairs. Linda (sister-in-law) came upstairs and gave me a tie for my birthday. Mandie and I watched a movie and ordered Chinese food for delivery (Snow Pea Restaurant in Lakewood — always use the same one). When movie finished at 9:00 took dog for evening walk (short walk to end of street — same every night). Came home gave dog his doggie biscuit. Got ready for bed. Probably watched TV through end of news but don't specifically remember. It's what we usually do every night unless we fall asleep. Would have been asleep by 10:30- 10:45. I am a very sound sleeper and do not remember waking up.

Saturday 9/21

Don't remember specific time waking up—would have been by 6:30 to make tee time. Walked dog and returned home to read paper. Probably left house by 7:30. Played golf at Sherrill Park No.2 course (Richardson public course) at 8:20 tee time. Played with Tom Robertson, Lon Berkowitz and Lon's father-in-law Teddy Gautier. Teddy was in town for weekend—lives in Houston (Woodlands Development). Shot 97—not very good. Remembered finishing quickly and being home at 1:00. Had told Mandie 1:30 but finished sooner due to relatively short length of course and Lon and Teddy having good rounds. Mandie was eating lunch and watching TV when I got home. She had not waited because she expected me later. I fixed myself lunch and watched the Notre Dame/Michigan ST Game with her on couch. She laid down and took a nap. I also took nap in La-z-boy during most of 2nd half of game. She slept on couch until approximately 5:00. I got up about 3:30 or 4:00. I mowed yard then walked dog. We bathed dog starting at 5:30 or 6:00 and finished at 6:30. Mandie, Linda and I went to dinner at 7:00 at Anita's Mexican Cafe (7324 Gaston Avenue). Linda had wanted to eat Mexican food for a few days. Credit card slip was cashed out at 8:53. We walked across parking lot to Block Buster Video and rented 2 movies. Returned to car. Stopped at a convenience type store across from restaurant and bought a 12 pack of Coors Light. Returned home at 9:40 and started watching a movie. Mandie fell asleep in La-z-boy and Linda said she was getting tired. Stopped movie.

Mandie went to bed. I walked dog and went to bed. Asleep probably around 11:00 to 11:15. Don't remember waking up during night.

Sunday 9/22

Awoke at 6:15-6:30. Mandie suggested donuts while we read paper. We get donuts approximately 4 to 6 weeks—definitely not a weekly tradition. Reading the paper together is. Mandie usually goes through the paper and sorts it by giving me sports section setting aside sections/advertisements that we don't look at. Mandie put on some clothes she had worn Saturday night as they were on floor by her side of bed when she had gone to bed. She left home at 6:45 to get donuts. Always get donuts at shop in strip center in northwest corner of Abrams and Mockingbird. I was getting leash for dog as she walked out. She had purse and I noticed nothing else. Don't specifically remember hearing car leave garage. Walked downstairs with dog and noticed newspaper had not arrived. Did notice garage door was up. She only leaves door up when gone for a quick trip. Door is always down when we are gone. Walked dog down Paulus around YMCA, up Tremont and home. Paper had arrived but not Mandie. Went upstairs and got cat and dog food for pets. Sat at kitchen table and started reading paper and having my ritual morning glass of orange juice. Finished sports section (usually spend approximately 15 to 20 minutes reading Sunday sports section). Thought it odd that Mandie had not returned but didn't really worry. Read comics and skimmed business section and became somewhat more concerned about Mandie. Left house and drove to donut shop to see if she had had car trouble. Her left rear tire (I think) had been having a slow leak and maybe she had had a flat. Probably left house at 7:45 and returned home at 8:05. Remember not having heard Linda up yet that morning. Called her (Linda) to see if Mandie had called. I think I woke her up or she was still laying in bed. She had not heard. I wasn't too worried because she had other errands to run. I told Linda I had to go to office that morning and have Mandie call me. I showered and shaved. I think I spoke with Linda again before leaving the house but am not positive. left house at 8:45 and arrived at office at 9:00. Used security key to go to office but had to ask security guard for some help as key at first did not want to work in elevator. Finished revisions to Zakcap Transportation proposal budget for Marvin Finks and modified draft of proposal letter. Left budget in Marvin's office and put draft back into typing. Had gone to office because Marvin intended to go over proposal with client on Monday and I was to be in Cleburne for a plant tour at new client (Acme Universal).

Got ready to leave office at 10:00. Called my house to see if Mandie had made it back yet—no answer and left short message on answering machine. Called Linda who also had no information. I had left a note on door for Mandie to call me at office when she got home. She knows my direct dial but I received no calls. All phones roll onto the night bell but did not hear the night bell. Was listening as I was in the computer room to use printer. Arrived home at approximately 10:15 to 10:20. Linda came out as I got to front of house. We talked briefly commenting on how it was odd we had not seen Mandie but we were not terribly worried.

Mandie intended to do grocery shopping (always shop at Skaggs at Abrams and Mockingbird) get fertilizer at Callaways (in Mesquite) and get something at Home Depot (in Mesquite). I don't remember what she was getting at Home Depot. Mandie is very particular in going through house and making a list before doing grocery shopping and I was not aware she had done that. She usually does it after reading the newspaper and clipping selected coupons from newspaper. Linda was going to church which is not usually the case but Bernard was receiving a Bible in a ceremony for first graders. I told Linda we would be at her parents for lunch if Mandie was back or for Linda to call me if we were not there when they got in from church. The three of us had discussed having lunch there when we were at dinner Saturday night. We were going because Carolyn Deer (Mandie and Linda's Mother) had made a special cheesecake for my birthday. Carolyn thought that cheesecake was my favorite dessert due to a telephone conversation I had had with [her] a while back. Linda left the house at 10:20. Started some laundry and started watching the other movie we had rented Saturday night. Worked on laundry and watched movie until 12:30. No word from Mandie. Linda called about then and we were very concerned. It was very unlike Mandie not to make an appointment—particularly when we had discussed it the previous evening. We have never missed a lunch/dinner at the Deers' when we said we would be there. Linda suggested I call the police to start a missing persons report. I called 911 and was given the number for the jail and Parkland and told to check there first then they would process a report. I called the jail but the computers were down. The jail said to call back in approximately 30 minutes and they could check. I called Parkland, Baylor, Dallas Memorial, Presbyterian , Saint Paul and Methodist. None had any admissions for Mandie. Called jail at approximately 1:30 and was told that computers were still down and call back in 30 minutes. Called credit cards (American Express, Master Card, and Discover) to check for any activity. American Express and Discover said there had been none. Master Card said I would have to call on Monday during business hours. Sometime between 1:00 and 1:30 Linda and Jasper Deer arrived at the house. They went back to the donut shop to talk to the employees but the shop was closed at noon on Sunday. I called the jail and at 2:10 was told that Mandie was not at the jail. Linda and Jasper had returned by then. I called 911 and asked to file a missing persons report. They took my name and number and said someone would call me back to get the details. Linda decided to go to Mandie's office downtown to see if she had been there. The building requires people to log in and out at the front desk on weekends. A security guard is required to activate the elevator on the weekends. A female officer called to take the report. I think it was between 3:00 and 3:30 but am not sure. The officer took the information, gave me a report number (1234567) and asked me to hold a moment. I was on hold possibly 20 to 30 minutes. During this time Linda had returned from Mandie's office. Jasper had been there since their return from the donut shop. I finally hung up and called back and was told Steve O'Donnell had been assigned and he would be in contact with me later in the afternoon. Jasper, Linda and I waited for a while. Jasper left at some point probably 4:30 to 5:00 to return home so he and Carolyn Could take the nephews to choir practice. Linda and I stayed at the house. Linda left approximately 5:45 to 6:15 to pick the boys up from choir. I am not sure of the exact time but I think choir finished at 6:30 and she would have allowed 20 minutes to drive to the church in Richardson. Linda returned with the boys at 7:30 (I

Think). I had walked the dog sometime between 6:00 and 7:00 because I remember 60 Minutes being on TV after the football game.

Molly or Bernard Morgonton picked the boys up sometime during the evening probably 7:45 to 8:15. Linda came upstairs for a while—not sure how long. The Deers called after returning home from church to see if there was any news. Sometime (I think between 6:00 and 8:00) I spoke with Steve O'Donnell who asked me some questions and said to call him on Monday at 3:30. I called my brother (James Frumpt) (I think between 8:30 and 9:30) to inform him of the situation. Linda had gone back to her house prior to 9:00 because I had walked the dog and finished watching the Cowboys game in bed. Tried to sleep but was very restless during the night. Remember the next door neighbor's dog barking early Monday morning (at 4:30 to 6:00).

Monday 9/23

Was out of bed by 6:30 to 7:00. Walked the dog and read the paper. Linda and I went to the donut shop at approximately 8:15. Talked with an Oriental man who had marginal English. He could not remember if Mandie had been in but told us his brother was also at the shop but would be asleep until 9:00. We returned home by way of Skillman to see if we saw Mandie's car. I called my office to speak with Marvin Finks about the situation but he was not in (time 8:45). Marvin and I have the same secretary. Waited until Marvin called me back (approximately 9:15). I think he was calling from his car phone based on background noise. Explained situation and he agreed it was very unlike Mandie. Mandie had worked at ABC Company from 1983 until June 1989 and Marvin knew her very well. After talking with Marvin, called Mandie's office and left message for Sam Pyland or

Will Taylor to call me. Andy Willins (a partner) called me back at approximately 9:45. Explained situation to him and he also commented on how un-Mandie-like it was. Linda and I returned to the donut shop at approximately 10:00 to talk with other brother. The second brother also had marginal English. He said he wasn't sure but in asking him questions we were not sure whether he understood us. We showed numerous pictures to both brothers. We left the shop and drove behind the strip center to see if we saw Mandie's car. Linda thought she had seen a brown car in the strip center on the northeast corner of the intersection. We drive through the center but did not see anything. We headed east on Mockingbird because I needed to return the movie rentals. When we got to White Rock Lake we decided to drive through the park to see if we saw the car. We started on the northeast corner of the lake and drove all the park roads around the lake. We got back on Grand (maybe Garland Road there at Buckner and drove to the Block Buster at Grand and Gaston to return the movies. We remembered a little park over by the projects and drove through that neighborhood and the park area on Grand and Samuel (connect streets?). We returned home at approximately 11:30 or 12:00. Linda needed to go to the grocery store and left the house about 12:00 to 12:30 (not sure exact time). I think Jasper called to see if we knew anything new — but am not sure. I was laying on the couch in a light sleep. Linda called about 2:00 that she had found Mandie's car at Lavista and Grand. I drove there immediately. Linda said the apartment manager had dialed 911 and a patrol unit was on the way. Linda and I looked at the car then searched the field next to the car. The patrol car arrived at approximately 2:45 (I think). They looked through the car and called a wrecker to have the car towed to the pound for prints. Officer Poole called the office to notify Steve O'Donnell who was not yet in. Linda returned home prior to the wrecker arriving. The wrecker arrived and towed the car. The patrolmen and I went to the motel located across Grand to see if they had seen Mandie. We had Mandie's driver's license from her car. The motel people didn't know anything. Officer Poole said there was a dirt road down Grand a ways where the police sometimes found stolen cars. He said they would drive down to the dirt road and look around the dirt road and look around the immediate area. Also a helicopter would be coming out to fly over the area. I returned to the house. Linda and Jasper were there. I changed into jeans and Linda called Bernard (her ex-husband) who said he would meet us at the car location when he got off work (about 3:30 to 4:00). Linda, Jasper and I returned to the field to look more. Jasper left not long after arriving. Linda and I looked up and down the railroad tracks and in two buildings which were gutted (located by the projects). We finished and returned to our car when Bernard and Molly (Bernard's wife) arrived. We knocked on some apartments located across from where the car had been found. Almost no one was home. The four of us looked around the apartment complex for awhile. When we were done we were joined by Sam (a friend of Bernard's don't know last name). We drove down Grand and found the dirt road running parallel with the railroad tracks and the White Rock creek/spillway. We walked the entire road but didn't see anything. Linda and I arrived back home at 6:00. Jasper was there waiting to get a picture of Mandie to make posters. I called James Frumpt (my brother) and he came over about 6:30. I called my parents to inform them. I spoke with Steve O'Donnell who said he would come to the house between 7:00 and 8:30. Linda, James Frumpt and I waited until 8:45. When we called the station we were told O'Donnell had left for the evening. Somewhat upset that he had made an appointment and had neither called nor come by we called back and asked to speak to his supervisor. I was told the normal supervisor was out and Detective Holt was acting Sergeant. I spoke with a Detective (not Holt) who said he had been to the pound with O'Donnell to look at Mandie's car and had not needed to come to the house as the car was unlocked. The Detective said to call O'Donnell on Tuesday about 3:00 to check on the status. I walked the dog with my brother. He left at 9:30. Lea (a co-worker of Linda's — don't know last name) had come over between 8:30 and 9:30. She contacted Jim Willett (Channel — —) about running a story on Mandie. We contacted Detective Holt to get permission. Willett spoke with Holt to get details while I drove a picture of Mandie downtown to Willett (approximately 11:00). I returned home about 11:15. Lea had contacted Marty (don't know last name) at Dallas Times Herald. I drove a picture to her and gave her the details on the case from approximately 11:45 to 12:30. A camera man for Channel — — had come over to get a copy of the picture. When I finished with Marty we went to Channel — — where I spoke with Carmen Velez. Returned home at approximately 1:30 and talked with Lea and Linda. Went to bed at 2:30.

Questions:

Went to lunch with Don Robbinson and Scott Smithfield (company staff). Ate at Dick's Last Resort (West End). Returned to office approximately at 1:00.

1. The three sentences above are known as ______________________________.

I am a very sound sleeper and do not remember waking up.

2. In the above sentence "do not remember" is an example of ______________________.

   Thought it odd that Mandie had not returned but didn't really worry.

3. In the above sentence "had not returned but didn't really worry" contains two examples of

   ______________________.

4. Examples of introjections were found _______ times throughout the narrative.
5. The narrative (does) (does not) contain an example of introjections related to his wife.

After the body of the individual's wife was found in a closet in their home, the individual was arrested. He then wrote the following narrative as an admission.

> I work at (company) and had been reasonably successful. I was promoted very quickly. I was promoted to manager effective August 1, 1990. I had always set my own standards, knowing if I met them it would exceed others' expectations. During the last year I had performed satisfactorily but could not meet my expectations. I started getting down and it seemed like a self-perpetuating cycle. The harder I tried to meet my expectations the more lethargic I became. In June or July of 1991 I decided to try and find another job thinking that a brand new situation would give me something to focus on. I mailed several resumes but received only one interview over a 2 month period. The interview went satisfactorily but I was rejected. The potential job was of a lower skill and pay position than what I was currently doing and still could not find something. I have never showed a great amount of emotion and even Mandie did not know I was as down about the situation as I was. Mandie, Linda Morgonton (Mandie's sister) and I went out to dinner Saturday September 21, 1991 at a Mexican food restaurant (Anita's Mexican Cafe, I think) and had some margarita's (3 each I think). We got some movies at the

> Block Buster Video. I stopped and got a 12 pack of Coors Light on the way home. We started the movie but we were starting to fall asleep. We stopped the movie, Linda went downstairs, Mandie went to bed, and I walked the dog. When I returned from the walk I started to go to bed but couldn't sleep. Mandie had laid down in bed, fully clothed and was sound asleep. I don't know why I did it and it was not something I had been planning but I started suffocating Mandie. I put my hands over her mouth and nose to cut off her air intake. She awoke with her eyes wide open in disbelief. She jerked some but I stayed on top of her for about an hour crying. When I had stopped crying I moved her body to the closet to the bedroom adjoining ours. I got [up] early Sunday and drove her car to where it was found. I dumped the contents of her purse on the floorboard and took the credit cards and cash out. I walked home and walked the dog, read the paper then called Linda to report her missing. Later I moved the body to the closet at the top of the stairs. The body began to decompose but I couldn't bring myself to move the body. I thought the detective smelled the body this morning when he came out to pick us up to get Mandie's car but I couldn't bring myself to do anything. Mandie was almost the perfect wife who I loved very much. She was not seeing anyone else and she loved me very much. I can't explain why I did it but have been unable to function since it happened. I acted alone and no one else was involved or had knowledge of it. I will miss her very much.

Compared to the first narrative there is a much more extensive use of the pronoun *I* in this narrative.

Please answer the following questions:

1. How is the use of the term *situation* in the second narrative different from its use in the first narrative?

Answer: ______________________________

____

____

2. Where do examples of negation occur in the second narrative?

Answer: ______________________________

____

____

3. What modifiers are used in the second narrative? What is their significance?

Answer: ______________________________

____

____

4. Explain the form of the narrative?

Answer: ______________________________

____

____

Summary

Semantic analysis involves a systematic search through the narrative for word choices which may be significant. These words are then examined and evaluated in terms of their isolated or consistent usage, as well as their placement within the context of the narrative. This semantic analysis provides the transition to the next step in the investigative discourse analysis process: *The Parts of Speech and the Analysis Process.*

Examination

The following two narratives—one from the reporting victim and one from the suspect—concern an alleged abduction and sexual assault. After reading both accounts, conduct a comparative analysis of the narratives. Focus on finding the linguistic components, narrative form, word count, and MLU. Summarize your findings citing specific linguistic referents.

Victim's Account

At 5:50 p.m. I left work. Went up the interstate and got off on exit 42, because of road construction. I got to the library at 5:45 p.m. or 5:50 p.m. When I walked in and looked around to see where I could sit down because it was crowded. There was a lot of high school students. And I believe I recognized a manager or assistant manager from the grocery store, but I was not sure. I stayed on the periodical side unless I needed to use the bathroom. I started my work. I went and got about 4 magazine articles and started making notes. Then I put them back and got some more but I made copies of them because it was around 8:20 p.m. He was standing at the tax papers then. I really did not pay him any attention. After I got my copies I went to look at and make copies of an article off the microfilm. After all that I went to the desk to staple my papers together. I went back to the table and packed my stuff up to go home. I can't remember where he was then. I left my book bag and coat at the table and went to the restroom. When I came back he was standing behind my table looking at new magazines. Then he walked out. I put my coat on, picked up my book bag, got my keys and walked out. This was exactly 8:45 p.m. by the library clock. When I got to my car I seen him unlocking his car. I unlocked my car turned to put my book bag in and he lunged at me. He put his right hand over my mouth as I was screaming, then he put his left hand with a knife to my throat. He also said he would kill me if I did not shut up. He forced me into his car then made me put my body in the floor board and my head on the seat before we left the parking lot. He drove it seemed a long time. I asked him if he was going to hurt me and he asked me what my name was. When I told him he said "Jane no I am not going to hurt you if you do what I say." He stopped and told me to get up and look out my window. We were at a fork in the road with a big oak tree on the left if you are coming out of the fork. In front of this fork there was a long, one story house or business or fancy horse barn with long, narrow window with black window casing. This is where he blindfolded me and tied my hands behind my back. He made me get back down into the floor board. Then we started to move again. Probably took about 5 minutes to get to the trailer. I could see a little bit under the black blindfold. We walk up 3 steps, turned to the right and walked into the trailer. He sat me on the couch, he left me there for a minute, then he got me up off the couch, turned me to the right and walked me to a bedroom. He said "no this ain't going to work," turned me back around and took me to a bedroom at the other end of the trailer. He told me to lay face first on the bed, he took the black blindfold off and replaced it with a white soft tee shirt, then he untied my hands. He turned me over and pulled me up into a standing position and told me to take off all my clothes. I asked him again if he was going to hurt me and he said not if I cooperated, he would not hurt me. I told him I had my period and he said o.k. I took my clothes off and he turned me back around and tied my hands behind my back. He laid me back on the bed and started rubbing my breast. Then he got up and told me he was "sorry." He said he was a sex addict. He said he was married and had a baby. He said he knew he could not go through with it. I told him I was cold and asked if I could put my clothes on, he threw a blanket on me. It got quiet and I asked where he was and he said he was getting a cigarette. Then he lit one and put it in my mouth. I sit there and smoked what I could and he took it and put it out. He told me I could put my clothes back. He told me he did not want to go to prison and asked if he hurt me, I said no, he said "I know I scared you and I wouldn't blame you if you went to the police, but I trust you since I did not hurt you." He said it was 9:45.

By this time we are walking out the door, he untied me but did not take the blindfold off. He put me in the car and let me sit in the seat. He just kept begging me to not put him in prison and I could only remember a right turn being the first turn we took. I saw more lights coming back and I heard more transfer trucks. He asked me if I went to the community college and I said no. He asked me what I was doing at the library and I told him I was doing a research paper. He said that he come in there for tax papers. He said he had not planned to do this to me but he could not refuse when he saw me. Right before we turned he made me duck down. We took a left turn and then another one and we were in the parking lot. He came around and got me out, he open my car door and told me to stand there, he got my book bag out of his car and I heard the zipper open then he said I could sit down, then he put his left hand on the door and pulled the blindfold off with the right hand and turned so I could not see him. He hugged me. He told me to lock my door and not to go out in the parking lot by myself anymore. I cranked my car and pulled out behind him to get his tag number. I left the library, went toward the car place and went up the interstate, went by my friend's to see if he was at home, he wasn't so I went to find the highway patrol station. I could [not] find it so I stopped at the BP, he told me a block down the road. I didn't see it so I stopped at Wilco to ask, and the lady asked what was wrong when I told her she called the police for me. Then the police came.

Analysis summary: ______________________________

____

____

____

____

____

____

____

____

Suspect's Account

I first met Jane at the library. I went to the library to get some tax forms. The moment I walked in I saw her. She was wearing her hair up with makeup and red lipstick. She had on blue jeans, tennis shoes and a pink or light red sweater. She always wore sweaters every time I saw her and they were loose or baggy. This was the first week of February on Wednesday or Thursday. I can't remember which. After I collected the tax forms I walked over to the magazine rack beside the table she was sitting at. I took a magazine from the rack and sat down at the table. She looked at me and smiled and I asked her how she was doing. That struck up a conversation. We talked about the weather, events around the world, the new president (Clinton), just normal small talk. Sometime during the conversation she had told me her name. I ask her if she was married. She replied “No, and thank God I'm not!” I ask her what she meant and she said “I don't like commitment, I like to date around with different guys.” I ask her if she had ever dated a married man and she said “no comment.” We talked and flirted for about an hour probably, then I left. The next time I saw her I had been thinking about her. I guess I became infatuated by her because I thought about going to the library more. So you could say the second time I went to the library looking for her. To my surprise she was there. This was the following week, I'm not sure of the date. I know it was late in the evening because it was dark when I got there. I walked over to her and said “do you stay here all the time?” She said “yes this is my second home” I said “I would like to take you home with me” and she replied “I'm ready, let's go.” So she started putting her books and stuff away in her book bag she always carried. It was a blue canvas type bag. We walked outside and she asked where was my car. I pointed out my car and ask her where was hers. She pointed out a little blue 2 door Chevy (I think it was a Chevy). The whole time I'm thinking am I going to get lucky with Jane or not. I was really excited and I think she was too. She said “let's take your car” and I ask her where did she want to go. She said “I thought you were going to take me home with you.” I said I would like to but my wife was at home but we could find a quiet dirt road. She said “let's go.” We left the library in my car somewhere around 7:00 p.m. We took the highway to the interstate. We stayed on the interstate all the way to the county road. We turned right on the county road and went to the second road on the left. This road takes you to School Road. We took a right on School Road and went about four or five miles to a driveway on the left. This is the driveway to the home of a friend of mine. We parked on the driveway. I didn't think he would mind. We had talked coming up the road and I told her about being married and that my wife would probably kill me and her if she found us out. I was assuming that we were going to have sex which we did. She said that she was engaged to get married in May or June and that it was the last thing in the world she wanted was to have him find out. As soon as we stopped on the driveway she asked me "do you love your wife?" For fear of her not wanting to have sex with me I told her that me and my wife didn't get along good and she stayed gone about all the time. Gone to see her mother. I then leaned over and kissed her on the mouth and we wrapped our arms around each other. We French kissed for about 5 minutes and she started rubbing my penis through my jeans and finally unzipped them and took it out. She told me that I had a big one and that it was bigger than her boyfriend's. She started taking off her clothes and we crawled into the back seat. It was cramped and uncomfortable at first but we moved around till we got comfortable. She was already completely naked except for her socks. She never took them off. I kissed her neck and breasts and finally moved down and performed oral sex on her. She told me I did it real good and I could tell she really liked it. I did that for maybe a half an hour, maybe not quite that long. We had sexual intercourse for about another hour. We both had orgasms. I know I did and she acted like she did. We laid in the back seat afterwards and smoked cigarettes and talked. That's when she told me she didn't want to get married.

But, she didn't want to hurt her boyfriend. We agreed while we laid there to be discreet when we met so nobody would know we were having an affair. I ask her if she had a number I could get in touch with her with. She gave me number 555-5555. I never used the number. She also said she came to the library all the time. She told [me] where she lived. I asked her why she didn't go to the library there. She said she didn't like the people who went there. We finally got back into our clothes and drove back to the library. We talked a few minutes and she (Jane) acted so depressed about us having to part company. I told her that I would call her. We kissed and she got in her car and I watched her leave. The third time I saw her I was already in the library reading some books and she walked up to me and said "hey lover." I turned and looked, it was her. I said not so loud someone will hear you. She said "I don't care I want you to take me home with you and keep me." Well I had felt real guilty about cheating on my wife and at first I took it out on Jane. I was mean and cruel by telling her if she didn't know how to act out in public that I didn't want to see her again. She just about cried and took off walking out the door. I should have let her go it would have probably ended then. But I didn't want her to be hurt so I went after her. I caught her before she got to her car. I told her I was sorry and that I was really glad to see her. Finally after I talked to her for awhile she pepped up and starting smiling and talking. She said "Let's go to your house and make love." I was kind of scared to take her to my house thinking a neighbor might see her going in and out and tell my wife. I took a chance knowing that my wife had an appointment with either a doctor that day or with the social services. So, this was early in the day around lunch. When we got to the trailer I was very nervous so I told her to lean down in the seat. I pulled up as close as I could to the trailer. We got out and just about ran in the trailer. The whole time we were there I was looking out the windows praying my wife didn't pull up. She (Jane) grabbed me by the hand and pulled me back to the bedroom. I was still looking out the window when I turned to look at her she was naked laying on the bed fondling herself. That was probably the fastest sex I have ever had. All I could think of was to get through and get away from there. We were there at the most 20 or 25 minutes. We rode around for a while after that. She kept on telling me that she loved me. I know I shouldn't have done it but I told her I loved her too. She kept on talking about us being together. She wanted me to leave my wife and get a place with her. It took a while to get away from her that day. She wouldn't let me leave from the library. She begged me for my phone number. I wouldn't give it to her but I promised I would call her. The last time I saw her was that March 1st about 8:00 p.m. The reason I had come back to the library was to get some more tax forms. I really wanted to avoid her. I had made up my mind to break it off with her. She was sitting at the table on the left of the library. I got the forms and walked over towards her. I stopped and said I need to talk to you. She didn't say a word, that's how I could tell she was mad at me. We walked out to the parking lot. When we got to our cars she starts screaming at me saying that I lied to her and I used her. I told her get in the car and quit screaming or I was going to leave. After a while she got in. We drove to my trailer. We went inside. By that time she had changed her tone and was asking me to make love to her again. I told her that we had to quit seeing each other. She got very mad then and started threatening saying she would tell my wife what a sorry low-down husband I was. She said she would go to the police and say that I raped her. I tried to be nice. I told her we could be friends. I didn't want to lose my wife and child. She finally said "take me back to my car." So we left the trailer probably about 9:30 p.m. She didn't say a word the whole way back. I kept telling her I didn't mean to hurt her feelings and that I was sorry. I guess we got back at the library about 9:45 p.m. We got out of the car. I came around the car and stopped her before she got in. I tried to hug her but she turned away. I said "I'm so sorry Jane, please don't be mad at me." She said "Go to hell, you'll be sorry, you S.O.B." She then pushed me away, got in the car and backed up behind my car. She sat there a minute just looking at me. Then she gave me the middle finger and pulled off. I left and I hadn't seen her since.

Analysis summary: ____

____

____

____

____

____

____

____

____

Chapter 5

The Parts of Speech and the Analysis Process

Concepts addressed in this chapter

Verbs
Pronouns
Nouns
Adjectives
Adverbs
Conjunctions
Prepositions

Introduction

As noted previously, the parts of speech play a significant role in the analysis process. In the analysis of word usage in any narrative, pay attention to every word. Every word is important.

Task 1

As you read the next portion of the MacDonald narrative once more, note the parts of speech and how they function within the narrative.

❖ Analysis Function: Verbs

Review the ***verbs*** that the individual used throughout the narrative.

Verbs indicate action or a state of being. Consequently, the individual's verb choices are indicative of the individual himself, the circumstances, or others.

- Are there places where the verb tense changes? What are the verbs? We have identified the tendency to describe past events with present tense verbs as viable opportunities for the application of questions in the amplification phase.

Answer: ____

____

____

____

- Are there places where the verbs themselves change? For example, does the individual use the verb *talk* in one portion of the narrative and the verb *discuss* in another portion? If so, is the difference between these verbs significant? And why did the individual select different verbs?

Answer: ____

____

____

____

- Do not forget each individual has his or her own lexicon. Consider how the operation of this particular individual's lexicon relates to verb usage within the narrative. If the verbs change, then there must be some antecedent that generates this change. Can you ultimately, within phase three, identify the antecedent?

Answer: ____

____

____

❖ Why did the individual choose a particular verb?

> Let's see. Monday night my wife went to bed, and I was reading. And I went to bed about—somewheres around two o'clock. I really don't know; I was reading on the couch, and my little girl Kristy had gone into bed with my wife. And I went in to go to bed, and the bed was wet. She had wet the bed on my side, so I brought her in her own room. And I don't remember if I changed her or not; gave her a bottle and went out to the couch 'cause my bed was wet. And I went to sleep on the couch.

Think to yourself, why, in this instance, did Captain MacDonald select the verb *brought*? What other verbs might have been selected? What verb would you have used? What is the difference between *brought* and *took*?

Answer: ____

____

____

Task 2

For verb usage of the same type, read the following portion of the vehicle accident narrative, noting the selection of the verb *bring*. What is the difference in the verb usage of *take* and *bring*?

Answer: ____

____

____

> I was unsuccessful in the attempt. I recall walking back to where my friends were eating. There was a car parked in front of the cottage and I climbed into the backseat. I then asked for someone to bring me back to Edgartown. I remember walking around for a period then going back to my hotel room. When I fully realized what had happened this morning, I immediately contacted the police.

Task 3

Read once more this portion of the narrative involving the vehicle fire. Identify each verb and concentrate on the full meaning and implication of the verb.

> At that time SGT Gary Regan 1/504 showed up at the scene. He also attempted. I ran to Mr. Turner's vehicle to see if he had water. He had a rag. I ran back and attempted to put it out, but the fire was unable to be brought under control. At this time I flagged down a vehicle to contact the authorities. The man in the vehicle agreed to do so. I continued to control traffic until the authorities arrived.

❖ Analysis Function: Pronouns

Review the ***pronouns*** the individual uses throughout the narrative. Within the analysis of discourse, pronouns can provide insight into the status of relationships and the labels the individual places on events, circumstances, and actions.

> Anne,
>
> Know you are very busy and don't have time for long conversations. We apologize to you for not getting back sooner and to explain why, considering it involves us, his employees. We called a friend in Admin-

istration at ________ and explained the situation to her. She suggested we just talk to you or send a narrative of events to explain things, so Jean and I are pooling our thoughts.

Task 4

In the narrative above:

- Who does "we" refer to?

Answer: ______________________________

____

____

- What is the "it" that requires explanation?

Answer: ______________________________

____

____

- Who does "his" refer to?

Answer: ______________________________

____

____

- Who is the referent of "she"?

Answer: ______________________________

____

❖ Analysis function: Nouns

Review the ***nouns*** used throughout the narrative, particularly those that refer to persons. Pay attention to the nouns used when individuals are first introduced into the narrative. If a noun used in reference to an individual changes, again, there must be an antecedent that has stimulated such a change.

Task 5

What referent changes can you identify in the narrative below?

Answer: ______________________________

____

____

> ... town and asked me to go through everything. Then my Dad, Lacy and James took me and put me in the car and went to Perkins. They ate I had coffee and cried. I went to Dad's and set there and cried, Janie came over. They called my doctor and got some medicine for to pick up at 9:00. My mother, sister Jina, Janie, Stacie wanted to eat so they went to Eatinplace and Janie said she would take me and go get my medicine and then would join the rest of them at the Eatinplace. Dad said Janie make her eat something before she takes that medicine. When we got there they order a gravy bis. I told them I didn't want anything but Daddy said you couldn't have that medicine unless you eat. So I took 3 bites took a pill and drank another cup of coffee. Went outside and at the car it come back up. Then went back to Daddy's laid down on the bed for 45 minutes. After that I can't remember what I did except going to bed at 12:00 or 1:00 that night.

Note how the father of the narrator is referred to as "Dad" and then the same individual is referred to as "Daddy." Although the person referred to (the individual's father) is the same throughout the narrative, something has changed in the relationship. That change is reflected in the words the individual uses as she develops the narrative. Foremost in the analyst's mind is the question: "What caused the relationship to change, as reflected by the use of a different term of reference?"

Answer: ____

____

____

Remember, nouns also designate things. As with references to individuals, when a reference to a thing changes there must be an antecedent which stimulates the change. For example:

> ... started to pick up the money bags. Then he said ...
>
> ... remembered the money. I had my back to Ronnie ...
>
> ... Tedd told Billy to put my money up in the bedroom ...

Note how "the money" becomes "my money." The change in designation acquires more significance with the additional information that these lines are from the individual's account of her activities on the day of her husband's murder. The husband was the co-owner, with his wife, of a restaurant-lounge.

❖ Analysis Function: Adjectives

Review the ***adjectives*** used in the individual's narrative. Because of the limiting or qualifying role of adjectives, their role in the analysis process is critical.

Task 6

Up to this point, we have learned that any change of reference terms used of persons or things (nouns) is important and has an antecedent, and that the limiting or qualifying role of adjectives makes their analysis very important. Combining these two elements, review the following narrative concerning a vehicle fire and identify:

- a change of reference to an individual

Answer: ____

____

____

- a change of reference to a thing

Answer: ____

____

____

On 21 September Approximately 1730 hrs myself and William Turner were on our way to Camp MacCall to retrieve personal items. At the junction of Chicken Rd and Plank Rd the vehicle ceased running. An attempt was made to start the vehicle. It was, however, unsuccessful. Due to a prior obligation I opted to leave the vehicle on the side of the Rd. The MP's were contacted in this regard. At 12 noon 22 Sept. I returned to the vehicle to inspect it and retrieve my wallet. At 1630 that same day I returned with Mr. Turner in his vehicle to attempt to diagnose the problem and repair it, leaving a tow truck an open option. I attempted to start the vehicle. It ran for approximately 30 seconds. I noticed the digital dash displaying strange numbers i.e. 35 mph and the car was standing still. After the car stalled I raised the hood to check the electric fuel pump pressure. I,

> therefore, left the key in the on position. As I checked it from outside the vehicle I noticed smoke rising from the passenger side compartment. I opened the door to investigate and at that time under the dash I saw smoke and small flames. I attempted to extinguish the flames with my hands. At that time SGT Gary Regan 1/504 showed up at the scene. He also attempted. I ran to Mr. Turner's vehicle to see if he had water. He had a rag. I ran back and attempted to put it out, but the fire was unable to be brought under control. At this time I flagged down a vehicle to contact the authorities. The man in the vehicle agreed to do so. I continued to control traffic until the authorities arrived.

❖ Analysis Function: Adverbs

Review the ***adverbs*** used in the narrative. Because of the verb-modification, the temporal, and degree-identification roles of adverbs, their analysis, like that of adjectives, is important. For example, pay attention to how the adverbs signal temporal lacunae in the following narrative:

> I had been at a party for approx. 3 hours when I had to go to the bathroom. **As I was walking** to the bathroom I started talking to this girl because we had to wait in line. She was looking a little drunk but so was I. She went into the bathroom and **when she opened the door** to exit I quickly ran past her in a hurry to use the bathroom. **As I was using** the toilet I noticed that she was still in there. **When I was finished** she started to rub my chest.

The following line includes an example of an adverb indicating degree:

> ... going on it was **just smoking around dash**. I did not see any fire.

Answer: ____

____

____

Note the modifying roles of the adverbs in the following lines:

> I had been at a party for **approx**. 3 hours when I had to go to the bathroom. As I was walking to the bathroom I started talking to this girl because we had to wait in line. She was looking a little drunk but so was I. She went into the bathroom and when she opened the door to exit I **quickly** ran past her in a hurry to use the bathroom. She said she was a virgin so I didn't continue for **too** long. I left the party **shortly** afterwards and was …

❖ Analysis Function: Conjunctions

Review the ***conjunctions*** used in the individual's narrative. The connecting or linking role of conjunctions makes them important to the analyst in evaluating the flow of the narrative, in identifying components which have been left out of the narrative, and in determining cause and effect. Instances of implied cause and effect in the narrative are particularly useful in determining the individual's rationalization process.

Task 7

Read Captain MacDonald's narrative once more and then answer the following questions:

> "Let's see. Monday night my wife went to bed, and I was reading. And I went to bed about—somewheres around two o'clock. I really don't know; I was reading on the couch, and my little girl Kristy had gone into bed with my wife.
>
> And I went in to go to bed, and the bed was wet. She had wet the bed on my side, so I brought her in her own room. And I don't remember if I changed her or not; gave her a bottle and went out to the couch 'cause my bed was wet. And I went to sleep on the couch.
>
> And then the next thing I know I heard some screaming, at least my wife; but I thought I heard Kimmie, my older daughter, screaming also. And I sat up. The kitchen light was on, and I saw some people at the foot of the bed.
>
> So, I don't know if I really said anything or I was getting ready to

say something. This happened real fast. You know, when you talk about it, it sounds like it took forever; but it didn't take forever.

And so, I sat up; and at first I thought it was—I just could see three people, and I don't know if I—If I heard the girl first—or I think I saw her first. I think two of the men separated sort of at the end of my couch, and I keep—all I saw was some people really.

And this guy started walking down between the coffee table and the couch, and he raised something over his head and just sort of then—sort of all together—I just got a glance of this girl with kind of a light on her face. I don't know if it was a flashlight or a candle, but it looked to me like she was holding something. And I just remember that my instinctive thought was that 'she's holding a candle. What the hell is she holding a candle for?'

But she said, before I was hit the first time, 'Kill the pigs. Acid's groovy.'

Now, that's all—that's all I think I heard before I was hit the first time, and the guy hit me in the head. So I was knocked back on the couch, and then I started struggling to get up, and I could hear it all then—Now I could—Maybe it's really, you know—I don't know if I was repeating to myself what she just said or if I kept hearing it, but I kept—I heard, you know, 'Acid is groovy. Kill the pigs.'

And I started to struggle up; and I noticed three men now; and I think the girl was kind of behind them, either on the stairs or at the foot of the couch behind them. And the guy on my left was a colored man, and he hit me again; but at the same time, you know, I was kind of struggling. And these two men, I thought, were punching me at the same time. Then I—I remember thinking to myself that—see, I work out with the boxing gloves sometimes. I was then—and I kept—'Geeze, that guy throws a hell of a punch,' because he punched me in the chest, and I got this terrible pain in my chest.

And so, I was struggling, and I got hit on the shoulder or the side of the head again, and so I turned and I—and I grabbed this guy's whatever it was. I thought it was a baseball bat at the time. And I had—I was holding it. I was kind of working up it to hold onto it.

Meanwhile, both these guys were kind of hitting me, and all this time I was hearing screams. That's what I can't figure out, so—let's see, I was holding—so, I saw the—and all I got a glimpse was, was some stripes. I told you, I think, they were E6 stripes. There was one bottom rocker and it was an army jacket, and that man was a colored man, and the two men, other men, were white.And I didn't really notice too much about them. And so I kind of struggled, and I was kind of off balance, 'cause I was still halfway on the couch and half off, and I was holding onto this thing. And I kept getting this pain, either in—you know, like sort of in my stomach, and he kept hitting me in the chest.

And so, I let go of the club; and I was grappling with him and I was holding his hand in my hand. And I saw, you know, a blade. I didn't know what it was; I just saw something that looked like a blade at the time.

And so, then I concentrated on him. We were kind of struggling in the hallway right there at the end of the couch; and then really the next distinctive thing, I thought that—I thought that I noticed that—I saw some legs, you know, that—not covered—like I'd saw the top of some boots. And I thought that I saw knees as I was falling.

But it wasn't what was in the papers that I saw white boots. I never saw white, muddy boots. I saw—saw some knees on the top of boots, and I told, I think, the investigators, I thought they were brown, as a matter of fact.

And the next thing I remember, though, was lying on the hallway floor, and I was freezing cold and it was very quiet. And my teeth were chattering, and I went down and—to the bedroom.

And I had this—I was dizzy, you know. I wasn't really—real alert; and I—my wife was lying on the—the floor next to the bed. And there were—there was a knife in her upper chest.

So, I took that out; and I tried to give her artificial respiration but the air was coming out of her chest. So, I went and checked the kids; and—just a minute—and they were—had a lot of—there was a lot of blood around.

So, I went back into the bedroom; and I—this time I was finding it real hard to breathe, and I was dizzy. So I picked up the phone and I told this asshole operator that it was—my name was Captain MacDonald and I was at 544 Castle Drive and I needed the MPs and a doctor and an ambulance. And she said, 'Is this on post or off post?'—something like that.

And I started yelling at her. I said—finally, I told her it was on post, and she said, 'Well, you'll have to call the MPs.'

So, I dropped the phone; and I went back and I checked my wife again; and now I was—I don't know. I assume I was hoping I hadn't seen what I had seen or I'd—or I was starting to think more like a doctor. So, I went back and I checked for pulses. You know, carotid pulses and stuff; and I—there was no pulse on my wife, and I was—I felt I was getting sick to my stomach and I was short of breath, and I was dizzy and my teeth were chattering 'cause I was cold. And so I didn't know if I was going—I assumed I was going into shock because I was cold. That's one of the symptoms of shock; you start getting chills.

So, I got down on all fours; and I was breathing for a while. Then I realized that I had talked to the operator and nothing really had happened with her. But in any case, when I went back to check my wife, I then went to check the kids. And a couple times I had to—thinking that I was going into shock and not being able to breathe.

Now I—you know, when I look back, of course, it's merely a symptom, that shortness of breath. It isn't—you weren't really that bad, but that's what happens when you get a pneumothorax. You—you think you can't breathe.And I had to get down on my hands and knees and breathe for a while, and then I went in and checked the kids and checked their pulses and stuff. And—I don't know if it was the first time I checked them or the second time I checked them, to tell you the truth; but I had all—you know, blood on my hands and I had little cuts in here, and my head hurt.

So, when I reached up to feel my head, you know, my hands were bloody. And so I—I think it was the second circuit 'cause it—by that time, I was—I was thinking better, I thought. And I went into that—I went into the bathroom right there and looked in the mirror and didn't—nothing looked wrong. I mean there wasn't really even a cut or anything.

So, I—then I went out in the hall. I couldn't breathe, so I was on my hands and knees in the hall, and I—and it kept hitting me that really nothing had been solved when I called the operator.

And so I went in and—that was in the—you know, in the middle of the hallway there. And I went the other way. I went into the kitchen, picked up that phone and the operator was on the line. My other phone had never been hung up.

And she was still on the line, and she said, 'Is this Captain MacDonald?' I said 'Yes it is.'

And she said, 'Just a minute.' And there was some dial tones and stuff and then the sergeant came on. And he said, 'Can I help you?' So I told him that I needed a doctor and an ambulance and that some people had been stabbed, and that I thought I was going to die.

And he said, 'They'll be right there.' So, I left the phone; and I remember going back to look again. And the next thing I knew, an MP was giving me mouth-to-mouth respiration next to—next to my wife.

Now, I remember I saw—I don't know if it was the first or second trip into the bedroom to see my wife—but I saw the back door was open, but that's immaterial, I guess. That's it."

Questions

1. The conjunction *but* is found in how many different times within the narrative?

Answer: ______________________________

2. The word *but* is an example of what investigative discourse analysis term?

Answer: ______________________________

3. What does its dramatic presence within the narrative indicate?

Answer: ______________________________

____

____

4. The conjunction *because* (or '*cause*) is found how many times within the narrative?

Answer: ______________________________

5. The word *because* is an example of what investigative discourse analysis term?

Answer: ______________________________

6. What does its dramatic presence within the narrative indicate?

Answer: ____

____

____

❖ Analysis Function: Prepositions

Review the ***prepositions*** used within the individual's narrative. Prepositions can give the analyst a sense of:

- the location or position of persons or objects
- the spatial relations between individuals
- the spatial relations between individuals and objects
- the spatial relations between objects

Note the prepositional phrases in this segment of a narrative, observing how they provide a sense of positions and relationships with regard to the victim and the crime scene.

> *I got home pulled* ***into the driveway*** *and the closer I got I saw something* ***in the carport****. Then when I got right* ***up on the carport*** *I saw Billy laying there, and the first thing I thought that I fell* ***out the door*** *and hit his and couldn't get up. So I got* ***out of the car*** *walked* ***up to him*** *and said Billy, Billy then I saw blood all* ***over his hand****. I touched him* ***on the arm*** *then I saw blood running down* ***between his legs*** *and I started screaming. Then I open the carport door, the t.v. was on. I saw blood* ***on the floor*** *and something shine like a knife and then I ran* ***to the living room*** *went to pick up the phone and it was* ***in the floor*** *and the head part was* ***under the coffee table****. Picked it up and dialed 911. After that I don't remember too much except begging them to help him. I remember sitting* ***in the police car*** *asking them not to leave him there and they asked me to take off shoes. I remember Bobbie coming* ***to the car*** *and talking to me. Then they took me downtown and asked me to go* ***through everything****.*

A Parts of Speech Analysis Walk-Through

We will once more revisit the narrative involving the vehicle fire for which we have previously conducted a partial analysis. Next we will add the examination of the parts of speech within the narrative to our analysis.

Task 8

Using the narrative and the narrative analysis outline that follows, respond to the directions and answer the questions. Sentence numbers are included.

1. On 21 September Approximately 1730 hrs myself and William Turner were on our way to Camp McCall to retrieve personal items.
2. At the junction of Chicken Rd and Plank Rd the vehicle ceased running.
3. An attempt was made to start the vehicle.
4. It was, however, unsuccessful.
5. Due to a prior obligation I opted to leave the vehicle on the side of the Rd.
6. The MP's were contacted in this regard.
7. At 12 noon 22 Sept I returned to the vehicle to inspect it and retrieve my wallet.
8. At 1630 that same day I returned with Mr. Turner in his vehicle to attempt to diagnose the problem and repair it, leaving a tow truck an open option.
9. I attempted to start the vehicle.
10. It ran for approximately 30 seconds.
11. I noticed the digital dash displaying strange numbers i.e. 35 mph and the car was standing still.
12. After the car stalled I raised the hood to check the electric fuel pump pressure.
13. I, therefore, left the key in the on position.

14. As I checked it from outside the vehicle I noticed smoke rising from the passenger side compartment.
15. I opened the door to investigate and at that time under the dash I saw smoke and small flames.
16. I attempted to extinguish the flames with my hands.
17. At that time SGT Gary Regan 1/504 showed up at the scene.
18. He also attempted.
19. I ran to Mr. Turner's vehicle to see if he had water.
20. He had a rag.
21. I ran back and attempted to put it out, but the fire was unable to be brought under control.
22. At this time I flagged down a vehicle to contact the authorities.
23. The man in the vehicle agreed to do so.
24. I continued to control traffic until the authorities arrived.

Narrative Analysis Outline
Sentence number:

1. 21 words marker word, non-confirming, generalized term
2. 13 words temporal lacuna, non-personal reference
3. 8 words* non-confirming, non-confirming
4. 4 words* non-personal reference
5. 17 words generalized term
6. 7 words* Non-personal reference, generalized term
7. 17 words temporal lacuna, non-confirming
8. 29 words temporal lacuna, non-confirming, non-confirming
9. 6 words* non-confirming
10. 6 words* non-personal reference
11. 17 words
12. 15 words temporal lacuna, non-confirming

13. 9 words* sentence out of sequence

14. 17 words temporal lacuna

15. 19 words non-confirming

16. 9 words* non-confirming, non-confirming

17. 12 words temporal lacuna

18. 3 words* non-confirming

19. 12 words non-confirming

20. 4 words*

21. 19 words non-confirming, abjuration term, non-confirming

22. 12 words temporal lacuna

23. 9 words*

24. 9 words*

❖ **Analysis function:** Record all occurrences of the pronoun *I* beside the corresponding sentence number above. What do you observe with regard to the positioning of this pronoun?

Answer: ____

____

____

❖ **Analysis function:** Record all occurrences of the noun related to the writer's mode of transportation beside the corresponding sentence number above. What do you observe with regard to this noun placement and usage?

Answer: ____

____

____

❖ **Analysis function:** Record all occurrences of the references to his companion beside the corresponding sentence number above. What do you observe with regard to this noun placement and usage?

Answer: ____

____

____

❖ **Analysis function:** Review the narrative with regard to the verb usage. As we have discussed, verbs show action or a state of being. Sentence 19 contains the verb *ran*. Write the verb *ran* in line 19 of the narrative analysis outline above. Now put the verb in context of what the teller of the tale is asserting. What inquiry cognitions come to mind? Think to yourself, "He *ran* to Mr. Turner's car. Where was Mr. Turner's car? Where was Mr. Turner?"

Answer: ____

____

____

Ideally, in a full, formal analysis, all of the parts of speech would be reviewed and the salient parts of speech listed on the narrative analysis outline. As illustrated above with the verb *ran*, the goal is to facilitate the analyst's deep thinking about what is there and to be able to carry the inquiry further. One question in the analyst's mind should lead to another. In this case, the question following, "How can I determine where Turner was in relation to the burning vehicle?" might be "Who can help me determine where Turner was positioned?" The answer to that question is "Sgt. Regan." Now, there is an additional step in the inquiry—meet with Sgt. Regan and have him write out a narrative describing what happened with regard to the vehicle fire. An example of a narrative-producing question might be, "Write out what happened from the time you arrived at the fire until the time you left."

Summary

This identification of the parts of speech used by the presenter significantly enhances the analyst's understanding of what has been said. This added knowledge sets the stage for the next step in the investigative discourse analysis process—the individual's amplification of the narrative—the interview.

Cumulative Examination

The following narrative involves the restaurant theft we have already discussed. Read the narrative once more and respond to the instructions and questions that follow.

> On Friday________, 20___ I received a phone call from David Jones, saying he was in Tenn. and wouldn't be in to work the next day. Tried to get someone to cover his schedule and couldn't. Went on about my business. Started paperwork as usual. Check everyone out in their areas. Everything was fine. Finished paperwork. Helped Dan Hartley dump trash, back in locked the back door, and pushed button in on

door. Mopped floor behind us, so it wouldn't be streaky. Came up to office, got my stuff together, straightened up. Set the alarm, closed office door and Dan and myself left. We punched out at 24:22 that night. When we got outside, Dan's ride was here, he got in the car and left. Pulled off parking lot about 12:30. Everything was organized and locked up when we left. Came back in about 5:45 am. Everything looked normal. Sandy Jones, Lane Taylor and my wife. We all walked in together. When we got to the door, to go in the back we looked on the hot cook table and there was some glass and a knife. I told the 3 employees not to do anything. I opened the office door and there was the $300 drawer, $950 bag and the deposit bag cut open. Everything was gone. I told the 3 employees to go sit in the dining room and called 911. I told them who I was and what happened. The only thing I touched was the phone. It took approximately 15 min. for the police to arrive. This all took place between 5:45 am and 6:00 am.

Respond to the following.

1. Number each sentence in the narrative.
2. On a separate sheet of paper number down the left side from 1 to _______.
3. Count and record the number of words in each sentence and place your answers on your separate sheet of paper.
4. Total the words from all of the sentences.
5. Divide the total number of words by the number of sentences to find the MLU.
6. The MLU is _______.
7. The central issue begins with sentence number ________.
8. The central issue ends with sentence number ________.
9. The pronoun *I* is found in sentences ________________________________.
10. The pronoun *we* is found in sentences ________________________________.

11. Summarize the narrator's usage of the pronouns *I* and *we*.

12. The following sentences were non-personal references:____________________________.

13. Sentence number ____ is a sentence out of sequence.

14. Sentence number ____ is an example of the historical present.

15. An example of a reference change occurs when __________________ in sentence __________ becomes _____________ in sentence ________.

16. An example of negation occurs in sentence _________.

17. Examples of the use of more generalized statements are found in sentences _____________.

18. The noun *everything* is found in sentences:_____________________.

19. The significance of "everything" is ________________________.

20. Summarize the placement of the parts of speech within the narrative and their applications to the analysis process.

Answer: ____

____

____

Chapter 6

Amplification of the Narrative

Concepts addressed in this chapter

Developing questions based on the document analysis
First question for a specific linguistic component
Subsequent question(s) for a specific linguistic component

Introduction

Once the semantic analysis of a narrative has been completed, the foundation for further inquiry has been established. In fact, it is the semantic analysis that facilitates the subsequent exploration and the manner in which it is conducted. This subsequent exploration is the interview process. The analyst incorporates the role of the interviewer into the process.

The procedure now becomes one of viewing the narrative with a microscope. In this manner the interviewer now will probe deeply into the elements the analysis has revealed. The interviewer strives to lead the interviewee toward an amplification or expansion of the narrative elements revealed during the analysis. Think of these narrative elements as windows of opportunity allowing the interviewer to peer ever deeper into the unknown. Negation, repression, temporal lacuna, non-confirming sentences, changes in referencing, and sentences out of sequence are just a sampling of the many windows of opportunity we have addressed in our analysis study to this point.

Those areas which a narrator may have wanted to avoid inevitably become the focus of the interview. In like manner, the elements a narrator may have wanted to minimally address and pass by quickly become the elements for which the interviewer probes for additional information. Ultimately, the value of the discourse analysis process becomes clear, as the interviewee is now confronted with the force of his or her own words. It is difficult to avoid one's own assertions during an inquiry whose foundation rests on one's verbatim word presentation. The productive impact of the interviewer's ability to quote, "David, you said ..." to the conduct of the interview is immeasurable.

The Amplification Process

The interviewer will decide how to proceed with the interview based on the narrative analysis. It is not necessary to start with the first window of opportunity in the narrative—for example, non-personal reference—and then go onto the next in the order they appear. Planning for the interview will entail deciding the order in which to open each window for the most advantageous interview outcome.

When initially addressing any one specific narrative element, ask an open, non-specific question. The two-fold goal is to determine if the interviewee will readily respond or not and, if there is a response, to pay close attention to the words spoken by the interviewee.

Do not place specifics in the first question related to an analysis element. Do not allow the interviewee to maneuver you into asking a specific question initially. Once the interviewee has responded to your initial, non-specific question on a given element, you can move into all of the specific questions needed on that element. However, when you move onto another element, once again the initial question is open and non-specific. After the initial response from the interviewee, you can ask specific questions. As a result, over time the interviewer can evaluate the areas in which the interviewee readily responds and note if there are areas in which the interviewee's resistance to answering becomes apparent.

Additionally, if the exploration of a narrative element begins to produce an emotive reaction on the part of the interviewee, do not feel compelled to move on to the next element. The emotive response may be the doorway to gaining compliance. Remember, ultimately, a critical function of the narrative analysis is to accommodate you in conducting subsequent interviews to a productive conclusion.

The following illustrates a series of amplifying questions corresponding to the semantic analysis components addressed in previous chapters.

❖ Amplifying Questions

The questioning of the interviewee following the analysis of the narrative proceeds along the following lines: "Bill, I have reviewed your account of what happened. There are some areas that I would like for you to make clearer or provide more details. Let me reference you to those areas."

As you refer the interviewee to the portions of his narrative to be expanded upon, emphasize those aspects to be detailed. (In the amplifying questions which follow, the aspects to be emphasized are in italics.) As you guide the interviewee toward the particular areas to be amplified, address the individual by name (i.e., "Bill," "Captain MacDonald," "Mr. Taylor," "Mrs. Smith"), using whatever form of address you feel is most appropriate to the circumstances.

Addressing the interviewee by name will help to gain his or her attention and keep the focus where you want it to be. Your emphasis on certain words in the interviewee's narrative will guide the process, and your non-specific, open-ended questions will allow the interviewee to answer freely rather than in response to any structure you impose. Ideally, the interviewer would use some means of recording the interviewee's responses so that this additional narrative material is, like the initial narrative, verbatim and suitable for subsequent analysis.

Using the analysis we have conducted on Captain MacDonald's initial narrative, we will focus first on his *lack of conviction about his own assertions.*

> And then the next thing I know I heard some screaming, at least my
>
> wife; but I thought I heard Kimmie, my older daughter, screaming.

Amplifying question: Captain MacDonald, you said "I *thought* I heard Kimmie, my older daughter, screaming," (go on, or tell me more).

" … also. And I sat up. The kitchen light was on, and I saw some people at the foot of the bed. So, I don't know if I really said …

Amplifying question: Captain, you said, "I saw *some people* at the foot of the bed," (go on, or tell me about that).

… anything or I was getting ready to say something. This happened real fast. You know, when you talk about it, it sounds like it took forever; but it didn't take forever. And so, I sat up; and at first I thought it was—I just could see three people, and I don't know if I—heard the girl first—or I think I saw her first. I think two of the men separated sort of at the end of …

Amplifying question: Captain, you said, "two of the men separated *sort of* at the end of my couch," (tell me about that).

… my couch, and I keep—All I saw was some people really. And this guy started walking down between the coffee table and the couch, and he raised something over his head and just sort of then—sort …

Amplifying question: Captain, you said, "he raised *something* over his head," (tell me more).

… of all together—I just got a glance of this girl with kind of a light on her face. I don't know if it was a flashlight or a …

Amplifying question: Captain, you said, "this girl with *kind of* a light on her face," (tell me about that).

… candle, but it looked to me like she was holding something. And I just remember that my instinctive thought was that "she's holding a candle. What the hell is she holding a candle for?" But she said, before I was hit the first time, "Kill the pigs. Acid's groovy." Now, that's all—that's all I think I heard before I, I was hit the first time, and the guy hit me in the head. So I was knocked back on the couch, and then I started struggling to get up, and I could hear it all then—now I could—maybe it's really, you know—I don't know if I was repeating to myself what she just said or if I kept hearing it, but I kept—I heard, you know, "Acid is groovy. Kill the pigs." And I started to struggle up; and I noticed three men now; and I think the girl was kind of behind them, either on the stairs or at the foot of the couch behind them. And the guy on my left was a colored man, and he hit me again; but at the same time, you know, I was kind of struggling. And these two men, I thought, were punching me at the …

Amplifying question: Captain, you said, "I was *kind of* struggling," (tell me about that).

… time. Then I—I remember thinking to myself that—see, I work out with the boxing gloves sometimes. I was then—and I kept—"Geez, that guy throws a hell of a punch," because he punched me in the chest, and I got this terrific pain in my chest. And so, I was struggling, and I got hit on the shoulder or the side of the head again, and so I turned and I—grabbed this guy's whatever it was. I thought it was a baseball bat at the time. And I had—I was holding it. I was kind of working up it to hold onto it. Meanwhile, both these guys were kind of hitting me, and all this …

Amplifying question: Captain, you said, "both these guys were *kind of* hitting me," (tell me more).

… time I was hearing screams. That's what I can't figure out, so—Let's see, I was holding—so, I saw the—and all I got a glimpse was, was some stripes. I told you, I think, they were E6 stripes. There was one bottom rocker and it was an army jacket, and that man was a colored man, and the two men, other men, were white. And I didn't really notice too much about them. And so I kind of struggled, and I was kind of off balance, 'cause I was still half way on the couch and half off, and I was holding onto this. And I kept getting this pain, either in—you know, like sort of in my stomach, and he kept hitting me in

> the chest. And so, I let go of the club; and I was grappling with him and I was holding his hand in my hand. And I saw, you know, a blade. I didn't know what it was; I just saw something that looked like a blade at the time. And so, then I concentrated on him. We were kind of struggling in the hallway right there at the end of the couch …

Amplifying question: Captain, you said, "we were *kind of* struggling in the hallway," (go on).

• Semantic analysis of the following narrative revealed the individual's use of many *generalized statements.*

> On Friday ________, 20__ I received a phone call from David Jones, saying he was in Tenn. and wouldn't be in to work the next day. Tried to get someone to cover his schedule and couldn't. Went on about my business. Started paperwork as usual. Check everyone out in their areas. Everything was fine. Finished paperwork.

The narrative did not explain why David Jones couldn't come in. ***Amplifying question***: Bill, you said, "I received a phone call from David Jones, saying he was in Tenn. and *wouldn't be in to work the next day*," (tell me about that).

The narrative did not provide information regarding whom "Bill tried to call. ***Amplifying question***: Bill, you said, "*Tried to get someone* to cover his schedule," (tell me about that).

What did "Bill" do as he went about his "business?" ***Amplifying question***: Bill, you said, "Went on about *my business*," (give me an example).

What "paperwork" did "Bill" start "as usual?" ***Amplifying question***: Bill, you said, "*started paperwork*," (tell me about that).

What does it mean to "check everyone out," and who is "everyone?" ***Amplifying question***: Bill, you said, "*Check everyone out* in their areas," (what do you mean) or (give me an example).

What was the "everything" that was fine? ***Amplifying question***: Bill, you said, "*Everything* was fine," (what do you mean)?

• Semantic analysis of the next narrative revealed instances of *negation.*

> Went to work I think about 8:00. Worked to about 7:30. Stopped gas station in Townsboro got some gas. Went to my brother's house took a shower. Went to My brother Scott Weaver's house in Turnville.

> Stayed about an hour. Left there went through Fremont saw a friend Peggy going in her house. Talked to her for few minutes. Stopped at my mother's house. Went in for a few minutes. Came back out got in car was going to my brother's house who I live with now. Smelt something burning thought it was ash tray. But it was not. Got to looking around saw smoke coming out around heater vent controls. Pulled over looked to see what was going on it was just smoking around dash. I did not see any fire.

Amplifying question: Bill, you said, "I *did not* see any fire," (tell me more).

- Semantic analysis revealed the presence of an *unusual verb* in Captain MacDonald's narrative.

> Let's see. Monday night my wife went to bed, and I was reading. And I went to bed about—somewheres around two o'clock. I really don't know; I was reading on the couch, and my little girl Kristy had gone into bed with my wife. And I went in to go to bed, and the bed was wet. She had wet the bed on my side, so I brought her in her own room. And I don't remember if I changed her or not.

Amplifying question: Captain, you said, "I *brought* her in her own room," (tell me more).

Captain MacDonald's narrative also contains an example of *repression*. ***Amplifying question***: Captain, you said, "I *don't remember* if I changed her or not," (tell me about that).

- Semantic analysis of the next narrative revealed *pronouns* having no obvious *referents*.

> Anne,
>
> Know you are very busy and don't have time for long conversations. We apologize to you for not getting back sooner and to explain why, considering it involves us, his employees. We called a friend in Administration at ________ and explained the situation to her. She suggested we just talk to you or send a narrative of events to explain things, so Jean and I are pooling our thoughts …

Amplifying questions: Mary, you said, "*We* apologize to you for not getting back," (what do you mean)?

Mary, you said, "considering *it* involves us," (tell me more).

Mary, you said, "*his* employees," (tell me about that).

Mary, you said, "She suggested *we just talk*," (tell me more).

When the analysis indicates *temporal lacunae* in the narrative, the interviewer's amplifying questions should be formulated as in the following examples:

> I had been at a party for approx. 3 hours when I had to go to the bathroom. As I was walking to the bathroom I started talking to ...

Amplifying question: Jim, you are now at the point *where you are "walking to the bathroom,"* (go on).

> ... this girl because we had to wait in line. She was looking a little drunk but so was I. She went into the bathroom and when she opened the door to exit I quickly ran past her in a hurry to ...

Amplifying question: Jim, you are now at the point "*when she opened the door to exit*," (go on).

> ... use the bathroom. As I was using the toilet I noticed that she was still in there. When I was finished she started to rub my ...

Amplifying questions: Jim, you are now at the point *where you notice that "she was still in there,"* (go on).

Jim, you are now at the point *where you just finished "using the toilet,"* (go on).

Whenever the individual has introduced an element of *degree* into the narrative, the interviewer should apply an amplifying question, as in the following example.

> ... who I live with now. Smelt something burning thought it was ash tray. But it was not. Got to looking around saw smoke coming out around heater vent controls. Pulled over looked to see what was going on it was just smoking around dash. I did not see any fire.

Amplifying question: Phil, you said, "it was *just smoking* around dash," (tell me more).

- Semantic analysis may also reveal *modifiers* that indicate something other than degree, as in the following examples:

> When I fully realized what had happened this morning, I immediately contacted the police.

Amplifying question: Ted, you said "When I *fully* realized what had happened this morning, I immediately contacted the police," (tell me about that).

> Following are some of the things I remember about the $212.00 missing from the Acme Child Center.

Amplifying question: Katy, you said, "Following are *some of the things* I remember about the $212.00 missing from the Acme Child Center," (what do you mean)?

> … both these guys were kind of hitting me …

Amplifying question: Captain, you said, "both these guys were *kind of hitting me*," (tell me about that).

- Semantic analysis will often reveal *prepositional phrases* requiring further explanation.

> I got home pulled into the driveway and the closer I got I saw something in the carport. Then when I got right up on …

Amplifying question: Linda, you said, "I saw something *in the carport*," (tell me more).

> … the carport I saw Billy laying there, and the first thing I thought that I fell out the door and hit his and couldn't get up. So I got out of the car walked up to him and said Billy, Billy then I saw blood all over his hand. I touched him on the arm then …

Amplifying question: Linda, you said, "I saw blood all *over his hand*," (tell me about that).

> I saw blood running down between his legs and I started screaming.

Amplifying question: Linda, you are now at the point where you "saw blood running down *between his legs*," (go on).

> Then I open the carport door, the t.v. was on. I saw blood on the floor and something shine like a knife and then I ran to the living room went to pick up the phone and it was in the floor and the head part was under the coffee table. Picked it up and dialed …"

Amplifying question: Linda, you said, "the head part was *under the coffee table*," (tell me more).

Amplifying questions should be employed in instances where an *out-of-sequence sentence* occurs in the narrative.

> I finished throwing the wrapper from my cigarettes away and turned to walk to the car when the man grabbed me from behind and began choking me and pushing me toward his car telling me to get in or he would kill me. When I was able to get a breath, I started screaming, and he pushed me into my car. I began blowing the horn. At one point I asked if he was a coach or a football team in town. He said yes then quickly said no ...

Amplifying question: Lesa, you said, "*At one point I asked him if he was a coach or with a football team in town*," (tell me more).

If the narrative shows a lack of human reaction or emotion, the interviewer can formulate questions to have the interviewee relate what emotions if any they were experiencing. Also, these questions can serve to produce an emotive response on the part of the interviewee. For example:

> ... my wife was lying on the—the floor next to the bed. And there were—there was a knife in her upper chest.

Amplifying question: Captain MacDonald, you are now at the point where you have walked into the bedroom and see your wife on the floor with a knife in her chest, how do you feel?

> Finished sports section (usually spend approximately 15 to 20 minutes reading Sunday sports section). Thought it odd that Mandie had not returned but didn't really worry. Read comics and skimmed business section and became somewhat more concerned about Mandie.

Amplifying question: You are now at the point where it is well past the time for Mandie to have returned home, how do you feel?

Task 1

The sentences below are from a narrative that we have seen previously. Develop an open-ended, nonspecific amplifying question for each of the analytic elements identified.

One night I had a visitor.

This sentence lacks specifics. The interviewer would want to know *what* "night" and *who* the "visitor" was. Write an amplifying question concerning the night in question.

Answer: ______________________________

____

____

Write an amplifying question concerning the visitor.

Answer: ______________________________

____

____

It was a friend or rather a relative.

It is the pronoun used for the visitor—a friend, then a relative. Write an amplifying question to address the friend-relative relationship:

Answer: ______________________________

____

____

He was from out of town.

Again, there is a lack of specifics: *Where* is he from? Write an amplifying question addressing the issue of the town.

Answer: ______________________________

____

____

And he came up for the weekend.

What is meant by "up"? Write an amplifying question addressing the term *up*:

Answer: ______________________________

____

____

When he got to the apartment, I didn't realize anything was wrong.

This sentence contains an example of *negation*. We learn that at some later point, the interviewee did realize that something was wrong. *What* was wrong, and *when* did the interviewee realize this?

Answer: ______________________________

____

____

Write an amplifying question addressing the subsequent realization that something was wrong.

Answer: ______________________________

____

____

I invited him into my apartment and gave him a mixed drink. Later on he went back to his car and brought out beer that he had been drinking.

"Later" is an indication of a temporal lacuna. Between the drink in the first sentence and the beginning of the second sentence, something has been omitted. The interviewer will want to determine that missing information. Write amplifying question addressing the temporal lacuna.

Answer: ______________________________

____

____

He also had a gun that he brought into the apartment. He proceeded to get very drunk.

Pay attention to the adverb *very*. *What* is meant by *very* drunk? Write an amplifying question addressing the degree of intoxication.

Answer: ______________________________

____

____

I eventually went to sleep.

Another example of a temporal lacuna occurs with the adverb *eventually*. Write amplifying question addressing the parameters of "eventually."

Answer: ______________________________

____

____

> When I woke up he was very drunk and there was beer cans and beer bottles strewn all over my apartment.

This is another example of a temporal lacuna. Write an amplifying question addressing the specifics of waking up.

Answer: ______________________________

____

____

> He was smoking a cigarette and using an ashtray that was full of paper. There was also cigarette butts in my carpeting. I started raising hell and at one time I thought he was going to get violent.

These sentences provide opportunities for several questions:

What is meant by "started raising hell?"

Answer: ______________________________

____

____

What is meant by "thought?"

Answer: ______________________________

____

____

When was the specific "time?"

Answer: ______________________________

____

____

What is meant by "violent?"

Answer: ______________________________

____

____

Write an amplifying question addressing "started raising hell."

Answer: ______________________________

____

____

Write an amplifying question addressing the time component.

Answer: ______________________________

____

____

Write an amplifying question addressing the term "violent."

Answer: ______________________________

____

____

> He started shaking me and wouldn't let me move. All I could think about was the gun he had brought in. I thought I was going to have to call the police to get rid of him.

There are at least three areas in the above that would lend themselves to amplifying questions. You make the determination and write the questions.

Amplifying Question 1:

____

____

____

Amplifying Question 2:

____

____

____

Amplifying Question 3:

____

____

____

Finally I just made him drink the end of the beer and I stayed up until he went to sleep.

This sentence has a temporal lacuna and an interesting verb. You make the determination and write the questions.

Amplifying Question 1:

____

____

____

Amplifying Question 2:

____

____

____

Task 2

Identify the bold-typed analytic elements in the following narrative and formulate an appropriate amplifying question for each one.

One night when I was sleeping I **thought** I heard a noise. As I was ...

Amplifying Question:

____

____

____

... waking up **this hand** came down over my mouth and **this man** started ..."

Amplifying Question:

____

____

____

Amplifying Question:

____

____

____

… telling me to be still. I **tried to scream** several times but he …

Amplifying Question:

____

____

____

… sat down on top of me and he kept his hand over my mouth. I guess I **kind of** went crazy. **We** started struggling. I bit his hand and …

Amplifying Question:

____

____

____

Amplifying Question:

____

____

____

Finally one of my **neighbors** came to the door. And he …

Amplifying Question:

____

____

____

Amplifying Question:

____

____

____

… started pounding on the door and the man got up and ran out the back door. **Later on** we called the police but they never found the …

Amplifying Question:

____

Summary

The amplification phase of investigative discourse analysis can serve to open additional windows for the interviewer. Amplifying the narrative guides the interviewee into those areas shown by the semantic analysis as opportunistic for further exploration. We can think of the initial narrative as an incomplete map. Analyzing the map provides information about both what is there and what is yet to be discovered. The amplification phase then allows the map to be completed so that the interviewer can use it to proceed toward the ultimate destination—the truth.

Examination

Conduct a complete analysis of the following narrative, to include a narrative analysis outline. We previously addressed the central issue for this narrative in Chapter 3. After completing the analysis, prepare a list of seven appropriate amplifying questions.

> I was standing in the back storage room talking to Missy Blaylock on the phone. A black man in his late 20's to early thirties came out of the bathroom and handed me a note saying — I have a gun don't do anything stupid or I'll kill you. — I got off the phone with Missy. He showed me the gun (medium pistol). He thought the money was in the candy room and demanded to go in. I took him in there and showed him around. He wanted to know where all the money was and how much there was. I told him. I also told him it would take 10 minutes to open the safe. He said to play it cool and open it while he waited. I set the timer and walked him around the store. After about 5 minutes I walked him back to the front, and took the money out of both end registers. I put the safe money together with it in a blue zip-perbag, then put the bag in a small box. I walked him to the back of the store. He left the box on the floor, put the bag up his shirt, then told me to walk him out.

Amplifying Question 1: ______________________________

____

____

Amplifying Question 2: ______________________________

____

____

Amplifying Question 3: ______________________________

____

____

Amplifying Question 4: ______________________________

____

____

Amplifying Question 5: ______________________________

____

____

Amplifying Question 6: ______________________________

____

____

Amplifying Question 7: ______________________________

____

____

Chapter 7

The Analysis Process and Alternate Forms of Documentation: Letters and Emails

Concepts addressed in this chapter

The analysis of non-narrative documentation

- Letters and the analysis process
- Emails and the analysis process

Introduction

Some inquiries involve the examination of a circumstance, relationship, and process rather than a specific event. As we have seen, the analysis of a narrative provides significant application regarding the inquiry into an event and the subsequent related interview. However, in other areas of inquiry—fraud, for example—alternate forms of documentation may be required. As a result, it is important for the analyst to have the ability to process alternate forms of verbatim written documents. As with narratives, the analysis can provide the vehicle for transitioning into the third phase—amplification. Those alternate forms addressed in this chapter involve letters and an email.

The Analysis of Non-Narrative Documentation

In the analysis of these forms of documentation, three elements are paramount: key terms (typically nouns), other parts of speech, and linguistic terminologies. By way of quick review:

- As in the analysis of narratives, pay particular attention to the presence of key terms, including their repetition and any changes in their usage.
- Verb usage will provide an overall sense of the action level in the writing. As previously, identify any changes in verb usage.
- Pronouns provide insight into the writer's perceived relationship to the circumstances described and the other persons involved.
- In addition to scrutinizing the information provided by the document, be alert to the possible absence of elements that should be included.

In summary, the analysis process for these types of documents is the same—the analyst must methodically process the document word by word.

Didactic Methodology Transition

In Chapters 1 through 6 we provided a comprehensive foundational analysis examination. The information provided, in addition to the multitude of tasks set before you, allow for a transition in our didactic methodology. As we progress from this point onward, we are going to apply a more Socratic method of instruction along with *you do it* exercises. Our questions and task-directing activities are designed to instruct you how to think about and process the document types. The learning curve will be better facilitated through the addition of these modalities of instruction. We are transitioning from one level to the next. In the event that you run into a term or concept that produces a mental vacuum, you can refer to the previous chapters to search for the solution. The mental vacuums and the subsequent searches for resolution are exercises for taking your knowledge and practice to a higher level.

The following letter was written by an individual who was subsequently arrested for the crime of fraud. This offense involved having a duplicate of a bank teller's stamp made in order to produce fake copies of deposit slips for deposits which were never actually made. Prior to arrest, the individual wrote this letter to the main office of the bank involved in the investigation.

Letters and the Analysis Process

Task 1

Read the letter and respond to the questions and directions that follow.

Dear Controller:

I would like to go on record to file a complaint against _______ Bank. This is a very long and detailed review on what has transpired on my account since January of ____. It is my sincere hope that your office can do something to help me in this situation and prevent this from happening to someone else.

I have two business accounts as well as personal accounts with _______ Bank. One is an escrow account for my real estate rental company and the other is my operating account for the same company. In January of ____ I deposited two cash transactions into my escrow account, one for $5,989.50 on January 18, ____ and the other for $11,298.00 on January 27, ____. These two deposits were done with other deposits on the same day. In mid February ____ they did not appear on my bank statement. I called _______ Bank and the person there told me it was a keypunch error and I was already credited for the deposit and they were sorry it happened. It would be on my next month's statement. I was having trouble with _______ Bank taking Visa/Mastercard credit card return deposits being taken out twice. I had spoken with Bonnie Smith _______ branch several times concerning this both in person and on the telephone. It appeared to be taken out twice.

Then in March I moved my office and I did not have a chance to review my bank statements. At the end of March I was preparing to take a 550 mile trip and the day before I was scheduled to leave I received a non-sufficient fund notice on my escrow account from _______ Bank of _______. I immediately called Bonnie Smith and asked her what was wrong with my account and my checks should not be bouncing, there was plenty of money in the account. I asked her if she was still taking the Visa/Mastercard credits out twice which could account for the errors. I told her I was leaving at 4:00 AM the next morning to please straighten this out that day or I would not leave until this was resolved.

Two hours later Bonnie Smith called and said I was right, she did take the money out of my account twice. She would return the money to my account, pay the checks, and credit my account for the bad check fees. She would have Sandra Parker-the branch manager help her. She told me to go ahead and go on vacation she would take care of everything here.

So I left. This was on Wednesday April 1, ____, on Friday one of my staff called and said Bonnie Smith called and said she did not make a mistake, they were not putting my money back and they were bouncing my checks. It was my mistake. I called _______ Bank of_______ to talk to Sandra Parker, she wasn't in again, so I talked to Bonnie Smith again, I told her I was coming back and would be in Monday to straighten the whole mess out. I came back Sunday—went to the bank on Monday with a list of all the checks I had written and Bonnie Smith had a bunch of deposit records and I told her to add up the checks written and compare it to the deposits I made. Leaving her with this list which I had placed my initials on the back side bottom corner on this list. Bonnie told me they were bouncing my checks Tuesday morning. I then called the main office of _______ Bank and they told me to take copies of all my deposits to the _______ office. If this didn't clear the matter up to call Mr. Sam Taylor of the_______office (the city Exec.).

I called Mr. Taylor and he assured me he would check into this matter. I got my receipts for my deposits and pulled my bank statements and made a list of all deposits. I made a copy of all my deposit tickets, again putting my initials on the back bottom corner of these copies. I then realized the two deposits were not on my bank statement. I went back to ______ Bank of _______ with all my receipts in hand and copies of all my tickets. I gave them to Bonnie Smith, the original deposit tickets, the two that were not on my statement, she examined them and told me she would send off for the research work and that would take 10 days to two weeks. I again asked to speak to Sandra Parker, she was not available again.

I told Bonnie Smith there was no reason for the money not being placed into my account, she had a list of every check and a copy of every ticket. I waited two weeks still no return call on these deposits. I finally got a hold of Sandra Parker and asked her what the status on my account was. She told me I had an altered deposit ticket. I told her we would see about that. I had two deposit tickets, one for $1,198.00 and one for $11,298.00. They were saying I placed a one in front of the $1,298.00 to get the altered ticket.

I called my attorney Janice Harris, told her the situation and she set up a meeting with Mr. Taylor at _______ Bank at _______. We took the original deposit receipts $1,298.00 and $11,298.00 as well as the $5,989.50 and others for him to inspect. He made copies in my presence. He asked us to give him 24 hours to either place the money back into my account or do whatever steps needed to be taken. We agreed to that this was fair enough. This was at 11:00 on Thursday, by 2:30 Janice Harris, my attorney, was called by Mr. Taylor and he told Janice the money would be placed back in my account by Friday morning, the next day, and I could go ahead and release my owners and guest money. He stated they had other problems.

I did not call the bank on Friday because I thought if they deposited it after 2:00 pm then it would not show up in my account until Monday morning. This would have been the third time I was told the money would be put back into my account. I decided to wait until Monday and then release all checks. Meanwhile guests and owners are calling and our office told everyone their checks would be in the mail on Monday.

Monday morning the FBI walks into my office, saying he is there to investigate me removing $17,000.00 out of my escrow account that I had gotten through a fraudulent deposit ticket. (What happened to your money will be back into your account?) I told him that was going to be hard to do considering I've been trying to get the money back into the account for over three months. I then went into the whole story with him. He asked if he could get the original tickets and I told him he definitely could but do it through my attorney. Janice Harris set it up for him to pick up the receipts. The FBI agent looked surprised to see the deposit tickets. The day before I gave the receipts to the FBI I took them to a documents examiner with credentials a mile long to have them analyzed. The report stated they were not altered and were original in every sense of the word and the stamp matched other deposits not in question.

The FBI calls back and asks for other tickets, made the comment I was probably guilty and my finances were bad and it all fits. Who's finances wouldn't be bad with $17,000.00 missing out of your account, part of it yours. I then received a cut and paste letter copy in the mail indicating there were two sets of stamps, which we already were aware but were unsure if the bank was supposed to have two stamps for the same teller number.

My attorney set up another meeting with the FBI to pick up the letter. She set up another meeting to pick up the other deposit tickets and Janice told me to bring every-one I had.

Sandra Parker had been to my office on three previous occasions, one of which she learned of the whereabouts of an extra key.

By this time my attorney is really concerned about the safety of my deposit tickets. So I took a couple receipts home with me, especially the ones the FBI wanted and I hid the rest in an envelope taped to the bottom of my desk drawer.

The very morning I was supposed to take all my receipts which could help prove my case. My office was entered and all the receipts having the larger print stamp on them was stolen along with $276.00 in cash. This of course makes me look guilty in the FBI's eyes. But these receipts could only help my case not hurt it, no matter which stamp was used it would not hurt me. So I took the receipts I had taken home with me to the FBI. We did not hear from the FBI except to say my finances were bad and it all fits. So finally the FBI set up a meeting between the FBI, the bank auditor Mr. Taylor, Janice Harris, and myself.

At this meeting we finally found out what was going on, there is only supposed to be one stamp. The tapes for the day's business in question were not available from the bank, indicating they no longer exist. So I asked them to pull the film from the cameras to prove the deposits were made. The film wasn't available either. I asked them to pull the original receipts and they told me they were destroyed. Conveniently while I was gone on my trip.

The copies of the tickets I gave to Bonnie Smith had been altered. This explained why Bank called the FBI. But if those records were altered then why did Mr. Taylor agree to put the money in my account telling us it was a bank error? They had those copies for over two weeks before meeting with Mr. Taylor. Why were the copies changed when I had the originals in hand and shown to Bonnie Smith. Why was the bank taking the word of copies when they had originals? I gave the originals to the FBI which created two problems for the bank. The copies of these receipts did not have my initials on the back my attorney knew about from the onset. The original deposit tickets I gave the FBI did not match the microfilm copies at the bank. They were done in someone else's handwriting. This is a problem considering I'm the only one doing deposits. I asked the FBI whose writing this was and he said the bank was having a problem with this also.

So now the FBI stated he was dropping the case because no Federal money has been lost. And even if the state's attorney were called they would not do anything because no Federal money was lost. And it was such a little amount. So I said what you are saying is I'm in a "he said" "she said" situation and I'm out $17,000.00. He said that was correct and he would return my receipts. So 5 months later I'm back where I started from and lost 20% of my business and still short $17,000.00. So my attorney contacts the state's attorney to start criminal charges against fund. They stated it was such a small amount but they would look into the case if I took a polygraph test to prove my innocence. I had previously refused to take one. So in order to pursue the case they had to give me a voice detector test because my doctor had put me on an anti-depressant medication because of the stress and strain I was under. I did pass the lie detector test.

Currently the state's attorney is involved in a murder trial and it will be a while before they can get involved into this case. My problem is I'm losing about 10% of my business per month while this is going on not to even mention the stress and strain I'm under.

Recently my attorney had me go through my other accounts to see if we could find other receipts with the stamp in question on them. I did indeed find three others, one fromNovember of the year before and two Visa/Mastercard receipts with the stamp in question that did go through the system and does match the microfilm. Both stamps were used by _______ Bank of _______ both before and after the receipts in question.

I have found someone else's account with both stamps being used credited to their account. I am currently looking for more accounts using both stamps. I will be happy to supply you with copies of all the following upon your request only under the condition no one sees these without my written consent or a court order. This is all the evidence on my behalf and I don't want anyone to have the opportunity to lose, change or alter any more records.

I will provide you with:

1. Copies of all deposit tickets in question
2. Documents examiner's report
3. Lie detector report
4. Copies of both stamped receipts, both before and after the questionable deposits
5. Copies of both stamps being used on someone else's accounts

_______ Bank also released information to the FBI without my permission or without a court order violating my right to privacy which is a federal law.

Is it normal practice for a bank to do the following?

1. Destroy original documents while under question?
2. Lie to their customers three different times about putting the money back into their account?
3. Not have tapes available for transactions in question?
4. Not have film from cameras showing deposits being made especially while in question?
5. Banks to give out financial information without customer's knowledge or permission?
6. Banks not filing CTR forms?
7. Changing customer's copies submitted?

8. Change customer original deposit tickets?

I believe I have covered the entire situation and will be happy to answer any questions you may have. Other than going to the state's attorney and perhaps going to a national newspaper with good investigative reporters my only other option is through your office.

I have only one other question, how does a customer protect themselves from this type situation, how do we know what is a legitimate stamp and which isn't?

I would appreciate any help your office can give. Thank you for at least reading this letter. I guess it would make a good headline

_______ BANK SWINDLES WIDOW OUT OF MONEY!

Sincerely,

Task 2

Answer the following questions regarding the narrative above.

1. Examples of introjections are found _____ times within the letter.
2. There are _____ different terminologies the writer uses to label this inquiry.
3. List the inquiry-related terminologies mentioned above:

___

___

___

4. The term *case* is found ______ time(s) in the letter.
5. The term *situation* is found _______ time(s) in the letter.
6. The term *mess* is found _______ time(s) in the letter.
7. The term *matter* is found _______ time(s) in the letter.
8. The term *story* is found _______ time(s) in the letter.

9. List the different terminologies in the order they appear in the letter.

____

____

____

10. What are the terms that reveal the gender of the letter writer?

____

____

11. What is the sentence wherein the writer inadvertently reveals the co-mingling of funds?

____

____

____

12. The term *account* preceded by introjections is found ________ time(s) in the letter.

13. The term *account* preceded by a marker word is found _______ time(s) in the letter.

14. An example of *negation* is found in the sentence:

____

____

15. The word indicating *immediacy* is found _______ time(s) in the letter.

16. There is a *direct reference* sentence in the narrative. That sentence is:

____

____

____

17. The most distancing of all pronouns is found _______ time(s) in the letter.

- The fraud triangle developed by Doctor Donald Cressey places pressure/motive at the left base of the triangle, rationalization at the right base, and opportunity at the peak.

18. What does your analysis of the letter reveal as possible pressure/motive for fraud?

____

____

____

19. Write an amplification question to address the sentence that supports your finding.

____

20. What does your analysis of the letter reveal as possible rationalization for fraud?

21. Write an amplification question to address the sentence that supports your finding.

22. What does your analysis of the letter reveal as a possible opportunity for fraud?

23. Write an amplification question to address the sentence that supports your finding.

Task 3

The following letter was sent to two employees of a medical doctor by an insurer requesting office records to support claims they had submitted for themselves and their families. The response from the two employees, which was written by one of them for both, follows the insurer's letter.

Read both documents and respond to the questions and directions that follow.

October 12, ____
Dr. Smythe
RE: Patient Name: Cindy Jones
Identification Number: XXX-XX-XXXX
Date of Birth: See Attached
Dates of Service: 01-01 ____thru Current Date

I am conducting a post-payment review of subscriber-payment. As part of this procedure, I am requesting supporting documentation for this subscriber's claim. Please send copies of the following records:

______Office Records

I would appreciate this information at your earliest convenience. A self-addressed envelope is enclosed. If you have any questions or require additional information, please call me at (XXX) XXX-XXXX.

Sincerely,
Anne Borden

The employees' response:

Anne,

Know you are very busy and don't have time for long conversations. We apologize to you for not getting back sooner and to explain why, considering it involves us, his employees. We called a friend in Administration at _______ and explained the situation to her. She suggested we just talk to you or send a narrative of events to explain things, so Jean and I are pooling our thoughts, first of all I think when you called the first time you talked to Jean and she said a "Cindy Jones" did not work there. The reason was that no one has ever been told our last names and during the past few weeks we have both gotten calls at home late at night and may have been followed. We have refused recently to fill some class III narcotic drugs to some new patients for illnesses they may or not have had. As the police have a tight lid on the street drugs and that includes pres. fills. So they turn to Dr. Office's.

Secondly, when you called again Jean's brother had just died after an illness of 2 1/2 years and was off for 3 days. Unfortunately for everyone, this put us even further behind. We did hire a lady to help out and then she didn't come last Thurs. and Fri. as her grandchilds were sick, but she was here yesterday.

Dr. Smythe has been and always will be an old-fashioned country family Dr. He works alone and doesn't like change or people questioning his doctoring. We have both worked for him for 19 years. Sort of like a family. A few years ago he offered us an Ins. pkg. with his _______ plan thru _______ instead of a raise. Jean's husband has _______ mine has _______thru Farm Bureau with his business. We opted for the raise. We checked then with _______ and was told then claims could be submitted to either Ins. as long as services were rendered. Didn't matter if patient was employee or family, it was legal. So this is what has been done over the years, periodically whenever there was time to do the paperwork. We spoil our patients. Besides our regular duties, we do all the ins. for all of them. I do MC and all HMO'S and Jean does title XIX, B.S., and misc. Ins. When we have the time. Ins., filing, and sending records for various reasons always are on the back burner for whenever there is time. Jean is the nurse and Lab Tech, and I do lab and office, etc. That is why some things can wait for 3-4 weeks (or longer!). Until this summer, none of us had charts in the office. Whenever any of us or our families were seen for one thing or another, he would do it usually early morning or after work or evening and weekends and one of us would note it on a slip of paper, toss it into Ins. basket and it would be sent to Ins. sometime. Mostly we wait and send in several at once as we are too busy with others. We are family and knew we did these services, so nothing more was done.

When and if checks were sent, he would deposit them or to be perfectly honest, he would sign them back to us or tell us just to keep them. (a bonus!) It depended on his mood and still does. We haven't had a raise for 5 yrs. by the way. So at times it was put on day sheet and deposited as a chg. and payment and other times it was ours. But Dr. Smythe does that with a lot of his patients, if he knows them, or if he knows they need the money more than he does, we write a tremendous amount of money for services off each month. We do not participate with M.C. or B.S. but we reduce and write off on an individual basis. That is why he is such a popular and caring Dr. He really does have concern for their whole well being.

In Dec. ____ he bought Dr. Paul Tuckerton's practice and 40 yr. old bldg. on 40th after he had a heart attack. It was a big move for us, especially since he doesn't like change. He keeps everything so we had a basement full of 30 yrs of med records and financial papers. Because of the age of the bldg. and over the holidays last year a water pipe burst and flooded the basement. Needless to say everything was ruined. We have just finished shredding all the financial papers for all these years and are starting in on some deceased charts. We thin charts out once a year and file them in boxes downstairs, as they are all soaked and ink stained and for all practical purposes destroyed. So even if records had been kept of all our families they wouldn't be legible prior to Dec. of ____ for most charts. We have a real mess down there and that is another of our frustrations, but again only Jean and I know the patients to go thru boxes and see what can be salvaged. Our accountant tells us not to waste time due to the fact that he has had such a successful practice and no one would be suing for anything anyway.

The only Dr. I ever saw make fewer notes and document worse was Dr. Tuckerton. He could have 30 yrs. of medical info literally on only 3 pages. So you see what we are up against. Even our patient charts only have a few words here and there. He continues to be a small town country Dr. who resists change, won't computerize and fights the ICD-N codes, CPT's, DRG's and any new restraint. Until this summer that is when he became the Med. Dr on the _______. Now he is aware of what can and is happening and not all Drs. and offices are like ours. But he still uses too few words and won't code which leaves something more for Jean and I to do for him. This is one of the reasons I just took copies of 10 charts from part of ____, ____ to present to FHP office to Daniel Rakel. He knows what he needs to do and still doesn't do it! Jean and I hope we can keep him legal and out of "paper trouble" until he wants to retire in a few years but it is tough!

Which brings us to our real message to you. Dr. Smythe and his wife are 2 of the most caring, honest people ever put on this earth. We are all a part of Christian families, but they would never do one thing wrong to anyone else for any reason. His ethics are beyond reproach and his reputation is spotless over the last 20+ years. Then Gov. _______ appointed him to a board several years ago and Gov.

_______ has him on one now, he has been Pres. Of _______ and _______, etc., etc. He does court testimony and he has thousands of patients who wouldn't move without his o.k. or take a pill or change anything. Jean has a large family living in and around _______, does church work with her 2 kids and is above reproach, sometimes being too honest with patients. As for me and my family we were born and raised here. Our parents live here and we will all probably die here. We literally have hundreds of friends all over town. Can't help but have after 47 yrs. I help several patients with other personal problems outside of the office, am a youth sponsor at our church and a lay minister. We are having a retreat at _______ Women's Prison next weekend. Our sons are about to graduate from the Univ. of _______ next May. They come home most weekends to work and see girlfriends as they can make 3 times in our city as what they can make in _______ on weekends. And it is hard for them, so they get their medical care here when they are home rather than student health on campus where you wait forever and send it in to _______ from _______. When they both graduate in May, they will be moving on and getting their own policies.

What this "book" has all been about is this: We know what some of these situations could look like since you didn't know us or our circumstances or the kind of office and patients we have. But as you can see we would have nothing to gain and everything to lose if we were not being honest and providing the services rendered. We all have spotless reputations and intend to keep them that way and would never risk them for anything. Our only fault was and is to be so busy with our patients and the massive paperwork for them that we neglected to keep our own records up to date. We are trying to rectify that now. We would be happy to give you any amount of references from people all over town to help you substantiate our credibility.

By way of this correspondence to you, we did not tell him we were going to get a little personal. We just felt it would help clear the air a little better. You sounded over phone to both of us like a person with insight and common sense to know what is right and fair. And that is what we have been with you in explaining this practice of Dr. Smythe's and our relationship to him and his patients.

Thank you for your time. We trust this is confidential correspondence. I'll call you later in the week to see if you have any questions. Dr. Smythe will be gone for a while with his wife out east. Jean had sent in quite a few claims also over a month ago and wants to know if these need to be resubmitted. We can do that now, as we have a few notes!

Respond to the following items related to the letter above.

1. Explain the use of introjections within the letter.

____

____

____

2. There are _____ different terms the writer uses to label this inquiry.
3. Those terms the writer uses to reference the inquiry are:

____

____

____

4. The term *circumstances* is found ______ time(s) in the letter.
5. The term *situation(s)* is found _______ time(s) in the letter.

6. Explain the use of *negation* found in the letter.

____

____

____

7. Explain the use of *immediacy* found in the letter.

____

____

____

8. The most distancing of all pronouns is found _______ time(s) in the letter.

9. What does your analysis of the letter reveal as possible pressure/motive for fraud?

____

____

____

10. Write an amplification question to address the sentence that supports your finding.

____

____

____

11. What does your analysis of the letter reveal as possible rationalization for fraud?

____

____

____

12. Write an amplification question to address the sentence that supports your finding.

____

____

____

13. What does your analysis of the letter reveal as a possible opportunity for fraud?

____

____

____

14. Write an amplification question to address the sentence that supports your finding.

____

____

____

Task 4

Read the following anonymous letter. Whenever conducting an analysis of an anonymous letter, the analyst should always keep in mind the question, "What would the writer of the letter had to have known?" Conduct a semantic analysis on the letter, searching for any and all of the linguistic elements found within the letter. Prepare a list of questions and directions such as those following the first two letters in this chapter. At the end of the letter, you will find space to list what inferences you can make with regard to the writer of the letter.

I hope you will excuse the anonymous nature of this letter. Whistleblowers do not do well here or elsewhere in our industry.

The purpose of this letter is to inform you of a great challenge to the honesty and integrity of Acme Power Station. This challenge is in the form of one Dan Baron. Mr. Baron cheats on his examinations in LORP.

This has apparently been occurring continuously since Mr. Baron arrived, much to our misfortune, over two years ago. Cheating occurred on his initial exams, LORP session exams, and annual exams. This cheating involves obtaining copies of written tests, JPMs, and conditions for simulator exams from file cabinets, desks, computers, and the simulator computer screens.

This appears to be known by many instructors and their supervision, and also by fellow licensed operators. Many have caught Mr.

Baron in the act of cheating. Those who told me they caught him cheating say they could not prove it, but, so many have caught him there is no doubt.

The most severe offense is that Mr. Baron may have also sold, or attempted to sell, exam information to other licensed operators. It was his bragging of this fact that led me to question others, over the past year, to discover the extent of his dishonesty. If one of us were caught cheating, or helping someone else cheat, we would have our license removed and face fines or jail.

There is no explicit code of honor among licensed operators to turn in such disreputable individuals; however, this must stop. This information will be forwarded to the NRC if Mr. Baron is not removed from all contact with Operations in the near future.

Emails and the Analysis Process

As we observe from the document below, an email is an electronic version of a letter written on paper.

Task 5

Read the following. Conduct a semantic analysis on the document, searching for any and all of the linguistic elements found within the document. Based on your analysis, prepare a list of questions and directions as before. Prepare a briefing of your analysis findings. Space has been provided at the end of the email for the list of questions and the analysis briefing.

Tammy Fay,

I received your email from Mrs. McDougle yesterday morning about "what happened to the money raised for the Ackmoid Health Association at Tucker Island in June."

For the past 3 years I have raised money here at Smithy Magnet for the AHA. My children have gone to/go to Tucker Island and I knew that Coach Bobbie had not done Jump Rope for Health in the past. When I saw that they were going to participate I asked Coach Bobbie if she would like some help. She is very appreciative since she had little experience with the whole event. She began giving me the envelopes with checks and money. I had exchanged small bills for large to make room and to be counted. The event took place on a Friday and when it was over I took the rest of the envelopes and finished counting the money. Over the weekend I finished the prize list and counting money. The day I faxed the list to the AHA is the day I took the pre-stamped, addressed envelope to the post office on Chickweed street. Without thinking I sealed the envelope with everything inside and put it in the mailbox. There was a little less than $800 in cash that I did not get a cashiers check for and the rest were personal checks written to AHA. In all, the total was $4985.

I talked to Sue and Lou (555-123-4567) at the AHA office several times. Lou said that the envelope could have had the old address and may have come back. I went to the post office to see if they had found the envelope, but it was not there. The last time we spoke she said that when the envelope was put in the mail that it was no longer my responsibility. I went by the post office 2 times to see if they had ever found the envelope. The envelope is still missing and has not been returned or found.

Please let me know what I need to do next. As I said before, I have been doing this for a few years and have never had any trouble.

Jane Smith

Summary

Letters and emails, like other forms of discourse, can reveal important information to those who are versed in the analysis process. These forms of word presentation, like the narrative, can reveal the author's goal in the words chosen to attain that goal. Again, the question to be posed as the guide will always be, "Is the individual's goal to convey or to convince?"

Examination

Read the following letter and conduct a complete analysis. Prepare a list of amplifying questions you would ask in the event you were going to conduct the subsequent interview. Hint: pay particular attention to changes in key terms. Space is provided at the end of the letter for the list of amplifying questions.

Dear Mary,

People will say that by my actions I am a guilty man. That I was a monster. That I was insane. But you know I would never have touched my children in an immoral way and my children know the truth. This I swear on my soul. My life has never been easy and I know that my paths are my own choosing. You and the kids brought me the only happiness I have ever known. I love you all dearly but I cannot stand this. To the people who hated me so, you can say they won. I just can't face the future not knowing if I can have my kids and you. I was not a perfect husband and father but I was no child molester either. Please find out who was. Tell Mom, Scott and Jane that I love them. But I have been broken. Under no circumstances let me be buried in the family cemetery. Cremate me if you have to. I don't care. My heart's too broke to care. I just can't deal with the shame of these accusations anymore. And you can tell Anne and Patty and Donna and the rest of your family that if there is a way to come back I will find it. I feel such hate for them it consumes me. I'm sorry. Please forgive me and as the God I will soon see is my witness I have never violated my children.

I loved you and my kids,

Tim

Chapter 8

The Analysis Process and Alternate Forms of Documentation: Transcripts

Concept addressed in this chapter

Applying the analysis concept to interview transcripts.

Introduction

The analysis of a verbatim transcript of dialogue provides an opportunity to gain additional insight from the interaction of two or more persons. Normally, in an inquiry, the transcript is made and kept merely as a formal record of the event—usually an interview or deposition. A detailed analysis of the individual's responses to the questions asked in such a context can allow the analyst to learn more about the interviewee and the situation, thereby advancing the inquiry.

In an ongoing inquiry, a transcript of either a statement or an interview should not be considered an end in itself. Rather, it should be considered a means to an end, a vehicle by which to help bring the inquiry to a successful conclusion.

The primary difference between the discourse generated by interviews and depositions and the other forms of discourse we have addressed is that the individual's words are produced in response to a systematic questioning process. Herein the individual must formulate a series of responses to a series of specific questions. Again, the analyst must determine whether the individual's goal is to convince or to convey. Each of these diametrically opposed goals can make its presence known throughout the discourse. In some circumstances, a transcript will display indications of both in different portions throughout.

Analysis criteria we have used previously will apply to this question-and-answer.

Task 1

We begin by analyzing the transcript of an interview with an individual who has reported that her home was broken into and that she was sexually assaulted. In the transcript, "I" refers to the interviewer and "S" refers to the interviewee. As you progress through the narrative you will find questions, blanks, and directions. Respond accordingly.

I: Tell me what happened from the time you left work. If you can start at that point and tell me exactly what happened.

1. The interviewer's use of a(n) ____________________ question allows the interviewee to initially respond with exactly what she wants to relate. An analysis of her response can then be conducted just as if she had written her response herself, as a narrative.

S: Well I got off ... I can't remember what time. I think it was after 3:00, and I stopped up there to the store and Mary brought me home and she gave me my bucket. I went in the trailer and cut on my lights and the TV and the man you met next door gave me kerosene because I didn't have no heat. I hooked up my kerosene and fixed me some fries and fixed myself something to eat, and I didn't lie to you Saturday night. I drank a couple of beers that night, and watched TV. I dozed off awhile, it was dark by then. Well no I didn't either. I packed some clothes up. Packed some of my suitcases and my boxes and stuff and I then went ahead and laid down and dozed off, and that's when I woke up ... and when I did that is when that guy was standing over on top of me.

2. From her response to the interviewer's first ____________ question, we note the following:
3. It took the individual ________ sentences to relate what happened.
4. ________ of those sentences comprise the prologue, or what occurred before the incident.
5. Describe the composition of the central issue in the response.

____

____

____

6. Describe the composition of the epilogue in the response.

____

____

7. The individual's allocation of subjective time indicates ____________________.
8. The contraction *didn't* is an example of ____________________.

I: What did he look like?

S: Tall, just a colored guy.

9. Explain the implication of the interviewee's use of the term *just.* ____________________

____

____

I: What was he wearing?

S: Jean coat, pants.

I: What kind of pants?

S: Jeans I believe ... I ain't for sure.

10. The word *ain't* is an example of____.

11. To this point in the interview, is the interviewee presenting a tendency to convey or convince? Explain your position based on the word usage to this point.

____

____

I: What kind of coat was it?

S: Like a jacket ... like a jean jacket or leather jacket or something. Anyway I felt the scissors on me and he said he was going to get him some. I tried to pull away and I couldn't cause he was too big. He was too tall. I was scared. All I can remember was my jeans were cut off and my panties were cut off. I ain't found them either. He grabbed his finger and rammed up in me. And he was messing around with fingers inside me and pulling my breasts. All I heard calling or something outside and when he left all I did was put my robe on and run next door.

12. In the previous answer there were _________ examples of introjections.

13. In the previous answer an explainer is shown with the word ________________________.

I: Okay. Let's back up and get some more details. When you left you went to the store. You were in the car with who?

S: Mary at work. I went and got me some cigarettes because I didn't have none.

I: You walked over there. Did Mary take you by there?

S: No, I walked. I walked over and checked on my trailer. The one I showed you this morning. Then I went on back to my house and didn't leave the house.

I: Okay. Then you fell asleep?

S: Yeah. I was tired because I didn't sleep none Friday night. And then I had to work Saturday. And I was wore out because I really hadn't have no sleep since Bill has been gone.

14. Explain the phrase *really hadn't have no sleep.* ________________________________

____

____

I: You woke up?

S: That's when I seen him and that's when I noticed the windows and stuff and I went to go next door because I didn't know where to go.

15. What linguistic elements are present in the previous answer?

____

____

____

I: Okay. When you went to sleep and you looked up and a man was standing above you and then he got on top of you and then what did he do? You've got to go slow and give me all the details.

S: Like I said he was playing with my breasts, pinching on them.

I: Okay. He cut your shirt off. Where did he get the scissors from? Do you know?

S: No. Now the ones I had I don't think he used them because mine was still laying beside the chair.

I: Okay.

S: And that's where I had them because I had cut off some shirts and a pair of pants of mine.

I: Okay. Do you remember what the scissors look like that he had?

S: No.

I: Did you ever see them in his hand?

S: No. But I felt something like it was cutting. I don't know if it was scissors, it might have been a knife. I don't know.

16. In the previous answer, "But" is an example of a(n) ______________________________.

17. In the previous answer there is/are ________ example(s) of negation.

I: So you don't know that it was scissors?

S: Well it looked … it looked like scissors … I mean the way it felt. It felt like … You know.

18. The use of the pronoun *you* in the previous answer is an example of _________________.

I: If he had the scissors … did you see what the scissors look like? You saying that you're not sure if it was scissors or a knife?

S: No. I was scared. I didn't know if he was going to kill me or …

I: What did he do with the scissors?

S: I don't know.

I: I mean what did he do with them when he was with you? What did he do with the scissors?

S: He cut my blouse and my bra off, and my panties were cut off.

I: How did he go about doing that?

S: Tugging … like he was trying to get them off …

19. In the previous answer, "trying" is an example of _________________________________.

I: I mean where did he start cutting at?

S: From the top of my … here.

I: He started cutting at the top and went down?

S: And then he got my pants off and then he got a hold of my panties.

I: When he started cutting didn't you look to see what was going on? You had your eyes closed?

S: Yeah. I was scared.... I was crying.

I: So you don't know if there was a knife or scissors? You didn't see them in his hand then?

S: I only felt them.

I: Did you feel his hand running down the side of you? In other words his hand had to be inside of your shirt?

S: Yeah. He was trying to get to my breasts.

20. Describe the linguistic indicators in the previous sentence.

____

____

____

I: So you felt his hand? Did you have a bra on?

S: Yeah. I had a bra on and I had my sweatshirt on from work.

I: Did he cut your bra too? So he cut your bra and your sweat shirt?

S: Yeah. My bra was cut. My sweatshirt was cut.

I: Did he cut your sweatshirt first and then cut your bra?

S: No. When he come down 'cause my bra hooks up in the front. So when he cut down my bra come down too, and come off, because I've got the kind that hooks right here.

I: So when he cut your shirt and he got to your pants then what happened?

S: He got them off of me. He got a hold of my panties and I begged him to leave me alone.

I: When you say he got them off of you, what did he do to your pants, your outer pants?

S: I don't know where they're at. He just tugged on them and pulled them like he was ripping them or cutting them. I don't know. All I know was that I was trying to kick and get away from him, but I couldn't.

21. Describe the linguistic indicators in the interviewee's last three answers.

____

____

____

I: What kind of pants did you have on?

S: My jeans like I always wear.

I: So you don't know if he cut them or if he pulled them off?

S: I know I got up the next morning and was trying to find my pants, but I was too scared to stay there.

I: Did you find your underwear? What did they look like?

S: They were blue, like little blue flowers, 'cause he left and I grabbed a pair that I had in a box near the couch and I put them on and my robe.

I: So after he … were you lying there naked? Did you have anything on?

S: No. I had my top still on, but that was it.

I: But he didn't do anything to you as far as intercourse?

S: With his hands and his fingers.

I: He put his fingers inside of you? In your vagina?

S: Yeah.

I: Did he say anything to you when he was doing this?

S: That he was going to get a piece of it. That he liked white women. And if I make a sound or say something I won't be there for long.

I: Did you tell these officers that the other night?

S: I think … I don't remember.

22. "Don't remember" in the previous answer is an example of _________________________.

I: Did you tell them the other night that he used scissors?

S: They felt like scissors to me … I don't know.

I: Are you sure you told them that he used scissors?

S: I think I did. Yes, because they took my scissors.

I: So you felt pretty sure it was scissors then?

S: Well you figured somebody is cutting down … you … you think it's scissors. They took mine, didn't you?

23. Explain the presence of direct references in the previous answer.

____

____

____

I: How about your pants?

S: I ain't found them.

I: Your pants and your underwear were both gone?

S: Well I didn't really look all through the house.

24. In the above, "Well" is an example of a(n) ______________________________.

25. In the above, "didn't really look" is an example of ______________________________.

I: What did he do after he took your pants off? Or pulled them off or cut them off you don't remember which? What did he do then?

S: Just that … he played with my breasts a while. Both of my breasts with his fingers, and after he left I didn't know to stay in the trailer or hide somewhere, or go to the neighbors.

I: Did he ever take his clothes off at all, pull his pants down?

S: No.

I: Are you sure?

S: Yes.

I: Can you tell us what he was wearing?

S: Just pants, and a jacket, I didn't see the shirt.

26. Explain the interviewee's degree of detail in the above.

____

____

____

I: Could you tell what color it was, apparently there were enough light that you could see things?

S: No.

I: You don't know what color it was? You're not sure if it was a blue jean jacket or a leather jacket?

S: It was a blue jean jacket or leather. I can't remember which one. I didn't want to look at him.

I: Okay. You're telling me that you didn't want to look at him and you're not sure if they were scissors or anything in his hand or a knife. You're not sure if it was a blue jean jacket or a denim jacket, but you're sure he didn't have his clothes off at all. You see what it sounds like to me?

S: Like I'm lying.

I: Well, I'm trying to get this out now. If there is something that you want to tell me, you need to tell me now, because I'm not trying to accuse you of anything, but if this ever goes to court all these facts will come out and if I can sit right here and find all these holes in what you are telling me in just a short time that I've been sitting here. What do you think would happen in court?

S: They would tell me I'm a liar.

I: Well, I'm not so sure that they would tell you that you're a liar, but what they're going to do is they will put you on the stand and attack your integrity on what you're saying.

S: What are you supposed to do? I mean you're scared to death and you don't know if you're going to live.

27. Explain the presence of direct references in the above.

____

____

____

I: Well help me understand. Help me to understand what happened, because what you're telling me is that you're not sure if it was a knife or scissors, and how he started at the top and cut his way down, and you said you didn't look. You wouldn't look at anything, but yet you're telling me you saw what he had on except that you're not sure if it was a blue jean jacket or a leather jacket which they are very distinctively different, and you said you're sure he didn't have his clothes off, but then again you can't even tell me what color the clothes are. Okay, now help me understand that.

S: I didn't pay much attention. I mean I noticed him there, I saw him there.

I: And you can't tell us anything about his facial features, or anything like that.

S: He was colored and tall. I remember him being tall.

I: How do you know he was tall? He was standing over top of you right? And then he laid down on you. He laid down on you and then started cutting?

S: No. He was standing up when he was cutting. Then he got down on the couch beside me.

I: You said that you went home and had a couple of beers.

S: Yeah, and ate my supper.

I: How many beers are a couple of beers?

S: Three or four or something like that, and then I had one left and I still had one left.

I: So you fell asleep then on your couch. And how were you awakened? What made you wake up?

S: I don't know I just woke up.

I: You just looked up and there was someone standing over top of you? You had the TV on didn't you?

S: I had it on, but I had it turned down.

I: You had the voice turned down. How close is your TV to your couch where you were laying?

S: Way over towards the corner.

I: Wouldn't there be enough light from the television set to tell you what color, what the guy looked like and what kind of clothes he was wearing and what color they were?

S: Not really, because my TV is not all that clear and I didn't have my lights on.

I: What size TV set do you have? About that size there?

S: No, it's a little bitty portable one.

I: Thirteen inch?

S: I think.

I: It's smaller than that TV there.

S: Yeah.

I: You see what I'm saying is I have a thirteen inch at home at it's all the way across the room and when it's on it lights up the whole room. You should be able to tell me what the man was wearing and what he looked like if you looked at him.

S: That's it. I don't know what he looks like. He was a tall black guy.

I: Do you remember if he had any facial hair?

S: What do they call them when they are real short like they greased down or something? You know like some of the colored guys wear theirs like real back.

I: Did he have any facial hair?

S: What's facial hair?

I: Beard, mustache?

S: No.

I: Are you sure?

S: I don't think he did.

I: How about glasses or anything?

S: No.

I: When you were here that night, when we talked and I asked you that same question you said you didn't know what to call it but he had hair like I do up above the lip.

S: Little bit.

I: So he had a mustache?

S: A little bit of hair here, but not down to here.

I: I just asked you if he had a mustache and you said no.

S: Well.

I: I'm not accusing you or anything, but the time I've been here talking with you and I see a lot of problems in what you're telling me. And I'm not even talking about the three different stories that you gave as far as you going home that night. Now, I'm starting to believe that you want some attention, and you want some attention because of your boyfriend. What's his name?

S: Larry. Why would I want attention?

I: Where's Larry at now?

S: South Carolina working.

I: Is he planning on coming back?

S: He'll be back Wednesday night.

I: This Wednesday? What does he do for a living?

S: Umm … drywall.

I: Drywall. Well, do you see what I'm saying? There are so many holes in what you're telling me. I mean I have done this kind of thing before. I have interviewed women that have been raped. I have interviewed people who have claimed that they were raped and I found out later on that they weren't; that they made it all up.

S: Well, I don't go around just getting cops involved or trying to make up lies and this and that.

I: Let me ask you something …

S: And I'm not going to lie … I honestly don't remember things …

28. In the above, "honestly" is an example of ________________________________.

29. In the above, "don't remember" is an example of ________________________________.

I: Do you take any type of medication for anything?

S: No.

I: None at all?

S: Except aspirins.

I: Have you ever taken any medication?

S: Well, I took heart pills a couple of years ago, and then I had gland trouble and he had me on pills for that.

I: How long were you on the heart medication?

S: I've been off of them … let's see I'm 40. I was about in my twenties when I got off of them.

I: When did you start on it?

S: I was about 10 or 11 years old. They said I had a hole in my heart, and I had gland trouble where it stopped me from growing.

I: Okay. Let me ask you this. Do you think that it would be conceivable that maybe you had a dream and this was all a dream? Would you like to think it was?

S: I'm beginning to think that I would like to forget about the whole thing. I don't know what to do. I think I just ought to let it go.

30. What is your assessment of the interviewee's answer above?

____

____

____

I: Well, let me ask you this. We want to do what is right. Okay, but you have to help us with this. You have to help us. If I can sit here and find this many problems with it that are unexplained that you can't explain, then you need to help me fill in the holes. The problem is a lot of things that you are telling me you are contradicting yourself on. You have been doing it over and over again. Now the man, when he broke into your house did you hear him break in?

S: No.

I: You just woke up and he was standing over top of you?

S: The only thing I had on my windows, because you can't lock them windows. Larry taped all the windows down before he left.

I: So you think he pulled the window open?

S: Yeah. Because they said that there was tape all down on the ground.

I: Yeah. On the outside.

S: Because you can't lock that window.

I: You think he reached in and opened up the door?

S: He may have. There is no way you can get through that window. You can't crawl through that window.

31. Summarize the linguistic indicators found in the interviewee's last four answers.

____

I: Well, you can't crawl through it so that is the only way he could have got in.

S: I'm sure I couldn't get through it.

I: Was your door locked?

S: I had the chain on, and I had the door locked because Larry told me when he left to make sure my chain is on the door. The back doors locked.

I: Could he have reached in and open up your door knob and then take the chain off?

S: He did.

I: There should be finger prints on the door then right?

S: Well, Susan's had her fingers all over the door when she came over that night.

I: Who?

S: Susan, the girl that I'm staying with.

I: Do you think that his finger prints should be on it, shouldn't they?

S: Not unless mine's on it.

I: What do you mean?

S: Because I opened the door when I went out and I was there that night. I had my hands on the door and the next day I was there.

I: Yeah, but you didn't open the chain did you when you went out?

S: No.

I: He had to open the chain to get in didn't he?

S: He had to because I kept my chain on the door.

I: So there has to be some prints on that chain.

S: Because anytime I'm at that trailer by myself I always keep my doors locked.

I: So there would be fingerprints on that chain, right?

S: Yeah.

I: If he touched it there would be a fingerprint here?

S: I chained it Sunday.

I: What?

S: I put the chain on it Sunday. You know when you guys brought me home and I went in and you guys left.

I: Yeah.

S: I chained the door then.

I: Yes, but they fingerprinted before then.

S: Oh.

I: They fingerprinted it right after we left. They fingerprinted everything. Our officers went in there and fingerprinted everything; the windows, the doors, the scissors.

S: Yeah. Because I remember somebody saying something and I told them that Larry's hands was on the windows and stuff because he fixed my windows.

I: Oh, well we can tell the difference with fingerprints. Let me ask you this, when he was running his hand down inside your shirt could you feel his hand?

S: Yes.

I: So he wasn't wearing gloves was he?

S: No, he had big hands.

I: How do you know that?

S: They were bigger than mine. You can about tell a man's hands when they've got them on your breast and stuff. If they've got little hands like mine or hands like yours.

I: Didn't you tell the officers the other night that he had gloves on?

S: I don't know.

I: The other night when I asked you the first time you said he did have gloves on.

S: Well the one hand he did, but he didn't on the other hand.

I: You didn't say that just a minute ago. You said he didn't have gloves on, that he had big hands. Now what did he do? Did he take the glove off and then put it back on?

S: He only had one glove.

I: Do you think it would make sense for a man who, if he was wearing gloves, he is obviously worried about fingerprints that he would only wear one glove?

S: I don't know?

I: Well do you see how it looks?

S: Yeah I understand. Can we just call the whole thing off? I think in retrospect I'm just going to have him take me to my mother's.

I: Well I want you to tell me what really happened, before we call the whole thing off. Why do you want to call the whole thing off?

S: Well you just keep on going. I get mixed up, I don't remember half the things that goes on. And if you guys don't believe me I know no one else will.

32. Summarize the interviewee's response above.

____

____

____

I: Well why do you think you get mixed up?

S: Afraid, scared.

I: Afraid of what?

S: I've always been nervous when talking about something, and then when I'm talked to again it seems like I get the stories all wrong or I forget something.

I: Okay. Well you see if it was minor details or something like that, then it is explainable and we can handle that. But these are large details like you seem to remember things that happen in your everyday life, but you've told me three different ways that you got home that night. You told me you walked almost to home and then you got picked up by Mary, and then you told me you walked a little ways and she picked you up. And then you told me that she picked you up in front of the building. You even told me that she stopped at the post office in one of your stories and in the other one you didn't. You told me that you walked and you could see him behind you and you kept watching him as you walked and then Mary picked you up and that is when he turned away. He turned away before you got to the high school and now today when you showed me the route that she took you home you said he turned at the road. And the other night when you spoke to officers you didn't say anything about someone following you when you were walking.

S: I don't know if he was following me or not.

I: Did you know that was him?

S: No.

I: But you said you saw a black male wearing the exact same thing as the black male standing above you. That was the description you gave me. You see that's three different stories. And at that time you were never under any trauma, there was no reason for you to be nervous or upset about anything. So those should be clear thoughts. Now when you get inside the trailer and you start talking about the other things, we can understand why there might be some discrepancies in your story. Why you might have only seen things. Even today during the whole time you have not told me one time how he hit you twice in the face, how the chair got flipped over, how the lamp got knocked off the table, and these were the first things that you told me when I got to the scene that night. You told me he was on top of you and he slapped you twice, he got off of you, walked over and flipped the chair back and got back on top of you.

S: I remember being slapped.

I: Do you know what I think? Now Linda, I think that you turned the chair over. I think you turned some of those things over that were flipped over because either you didn't think that the officers would believe what you were saying without something like that happening or because you wanted to make it look like a rape had occurred. Why were your pants not found? Why would the man take and run out of your house without doing anything other than putting his finger in you, run out of the house and take your pants with him? Which would definitely incriminate him?

S: Why would I do it?

33. Evaluate the interviewee's lack of specific denial at this point.

____

____

____

I: You tell me. You tell me why you would do it.

S: I didn't do it.

I: You didn't stage any of this?

S: No I did not.

I: Then why are you telling these different stories?

S: I didn't do it.

I: Why are you telling these different stories?

S: I'm confused. I'm mixed up right now.

I: I understand that. It's easy to understand that if you've been through something dramatic that you would forget details.

S: Do you think that I've done it to get like you said attention from Larry, because he is gone? I guess you all think it. No I know Larry is coming back and I know he loves me. I have no reason to be worried about him being on a job or being gone, because I know he'll be back. Because he planned on a big Thanksgiving dinner for us on Thursday.

I: You miss him don't you?

S: Yeah, but I know he is all right. He is with Susan's husband.

I: How long has he been gone?

S: Since Tuesday.

I: Last Tuesday.

S: Yeah. They've called every other night at Susan's house.

I: When was the last time that he called?

S: Last night.

I: And when was the time before that?

S: Tuesday night and then Bill called Thursday night.

I: Remember telling me that neither one had called Wednesday or Thursday and that you knew …

S: No, they called Tuesday night, but I thought that they didn't call, because you see I didn't stay with Susan most of the night. But Susan told me Friday when I talked to her that Bill called. Larry don't call, 'cause Larry knows that I was staying at my trailer.

I: But you told me Saturday night that neither one had called in three days because they would call tonight. You knew that he would call his wife tonight because he hadn't called in three days and you knew.

S: Well I didn't think they called. Susan said they did.

I: Yeah, but you told me that and you told me that you knew as soon as Larry had heard what happened that he would come home.

S: I know it. That is the reason why I won't tell him. I don't know to tell him now or not. I don't know.

I: You want him to come home?

S: He'll be home tomorrow or Wednesday.

I: Did you want him to come home the other night?

S: No, because I knew he wouldn't be back.

I: But you want him to come back didn't you? Did you want him to be with you?

S: Yeah, I never want him to go away from me.

I: Yeah, but you wanted him to be with you didn't you?

S: Well, what woman wouldn't want her man with her, but the man's got a job to do. You can't stand in the way because I've got my own job.

34. How would you evaluate the interviewee's response in the above?

____

____

____

I: Do you remember telling me that if he couldn't find work there you wanted him to come on back and you would take on extra jobs until he could find jobs and stuff?

S: I would work three jobs if he came back. If he could find work, because I love him.

I: Would you rather have him at home with you trying to find work rather than working up there and you would have worked and paid the bills and kept things going?

S: Yeah.

I: So you would work three jobs for him if he would just come home?

S: I would have, but I'm not going to stand in his way. Larry is the type, I don't know if you guys know him or not, he is the type that he wants to work. He doesn't want me to work.

I: I understand, but what you're telling me is that you would do just about anything for him to be home including working three jobs.

S: Now working three jobs or something like that, yes I would. But going around trying to call police and tearing up my house …

I: Let me ask you something. Did you call the police?

S: No.

I: Did you want the police called at the very beginning?

S: I didn't even know nothing about the police. The only thing I wanted was to be with my neighbors.

I: Who called the police?

S: I think one of them over there when I ran over to the house.

I: You didn't ask them to call did you? Did you think they were going to call?

S: No, I didn't know it.

I: You had no intention for the police to be called? Really what you wanted was for Larry to be called so he would come home.

S: No, because they didn't know where he was.

I: You wanted them to call Larry so that he would come home because you knew that he was going to call didn't you? And you wanted him to come home. Linda, if that is what's happening, that's okay. All you have to do is tell me. It's okay. If you made any of this up it's all right to tell me, but tell me now so if we pick up a suspect and we charge him with something like this you can ruin a person's life. Even if he is not convicted. So if you made any part of this up you need to tell me. It's all right. I understand. I've seen this before. I understand that people do this. It just shows how much you love Larry. Do you love Larry enough to say something like that?

S: Maybe.

I: I think you do. I think you love him a lot, don't you? All you really wanted was for him to come home. You didn't really want us to get involved did you? Did you stage some of this stuff? It's all right. Did you make it up, Linda? Nothing ever happened did it?

S: No. I guess I can go to jail now.

I: Go to jail for what?

S: Doing something stupid.

I: No, I just needed to know the truth, before it gets too far.

S: Yeah.

I: So you are telling me that nothing ever happened that night. You made the whole story up?

S: No one was supposed to know. The cops weren't to be called.

I: So the cops weren't supposed to be called?

S: Now I feel like a fool.

I: Don't you feel better now that the truth is out?

S: You think I can go back to work?

I: The only people who are going to know about this is us okay? What you tell your friends and what you tell your boyfriend is your business okay?

S: I still think I'm going to do what I said I was going to do.

I: What's that?

S: I think I'm going to get Larry to take me home to my Mamma's for a while.

I: Where does your mom live at?

S: Virginia. I think it would be best.

I: Were you just alone? You were lonely and you wanted him to come home. Is that why you went and did this?

S: Yes.

I: I've got to ask you one thing. We have to clear something else up, because it is something we have to do in an investigation, anytime we find someone who has been like this. Did you make up the story about your father too?

S: No, that was the truth.

I: Did he ever go to court actually?

S: Oh yeah.

I: Was he ever convicted?

S: No, because I was on heart pills and medication. I was young.

I: Okay, we just want to make sure.

S: They knew I'd been touched, but he went to court and he told them that I was losing my mind because I was on all kinds of medication. I do crazy things, and they let him go. My mother divorced him and left him.

I: We are not going to pursue anything. Whatever you want to tell your friends and people at work, that's fine. But let me tell you this. If it gets out in the public and they want to know what we are doing about this rape case, we are going to have to tell them that there was no rape. Okay? Because the press and people have a right to know what goes on. We are not going to tell anybody, but if they ask us, we have to tell them. Do you understand that?

S: Well, if they ask me, I'm just going to say that I've changed my mind. I'm going to drop it. I'm going to get my nose into work and go back home and get my life together.

I: Okay. That's it.

Interview Summary

Within this interview, the interviewee frequently used such phrases as *don't know*, as well as direct references. The interviewee related more about what she didn't know than what she actually did know about the alleged incident. This emphasis on "what I don't know" is to be expected when, as we suspected from our initial analysis of her first response and as we learned from her ultimate confession, the incident never happened.

Additionally, her use of direct references indicated a desire to shift the emphasis from herself to others. Finally, her lack of detail and specificity was another indication that the individual's goal was less to convey than to provide only what was necessary to convince.

Task 2

Read the following interview transcript and follow the directions at the end.

I: On the day of the fire, I believe it was Friday, is that right?

S: Yeah, yeah last Friday.

I: I want you to start from the time you woke up and just keep going until I tell you to stop. Tell me what you did from the time you woke up that morning.

S: All right. Uh, well I got up and uh, took a shower and got my clothes on and uh, I set the alarm uh, for my wife 'cause we had to take Tim to a doctor appointment at 11 o'clock in Pinehurst. So I set the alarm where she can get up and uh and I just smoke me a couple of cigarettes and sort of looked out the back window waiting for Dan to come up here and pick me up and then when I seen him coming up, you know I just come on out and lock the house up and everything.

I: What time was this?

S: Uh … I don't know. It was between 7 and 7:30. Uh I ain't got no clock in the living room and uh … anyway we was gonna ride around and look at some buildings and uh you know. Mainly I just talking to him about you know when I might be able to start work and what them people up there in Asheboro told him and stuff like that. I told that the Blackstone building was empty and uh you know asked him if he wanted to ride through the parking lot and look at it on his way up. So we rode up there, drove through the parking lot and uh you know rode around behind it and sort of looked at the building and uh left there and rode up to Sea Grove and uh … I don't know which way we went then you know. I don't know them roads up there. Went up to Sea Grove and he said something about … He said uh, something about a building being on down a road down there somewhere. But it was one that Bruce Jones owned so we didn't bother looking at it. And come on left and come back and uh, he said he was going, you know, said he knowed a building over at Eagle Springs where he used to work. Anyway he used to build there or something at one time. And uh, we come on back to the … to his house and uh, you know. He was going, you know, took me back there to the dog lot. We walked down there and you know, talked about his dog and stuff like that and him going on vacation. And he told me when he went on vacation, he wanted me to come down there and feed his dog every day. And cats and … and you know, mow and stuff like that and keep it up. And said he'd help me out with a little bit of money. If I'd do that for him until I could get the work and uh … So we left there and went on up to Eagle Springs. And … he showed … showed me where to turn.

Where that building was. We went down there and uh, built well. It was all growed up and everything. We didn't even get out of the car. I just circled around through there. And uh, then he told me to go up to that station up there. It was on up above where we went to the building. So I drove up there and we pulled in at the gas pumps and he gave me $10.00 for gas. And I went in and paid for the gas and come back out. And then we drove back here and he dropped me off. And uh, I went ahead and got my wife and Tim up and told her to hurry up and get ready and take him to the doctor. And we went to Pinehurst and took Tim to the doctor. And uh, and uh after we took Tim to Pinehurst, uh, we went to Asheboro because Anne was supposed to get her check at where she works. Well she didn't work none last week. She decided to quit and we had to go up there and get her check. Then when we got up there, they told us that they hadn't deposited the money in the bank and it'd be 2 o'clock before she could get it. So we went to the mall and got something to eat and went back and got her check. And while she was in there getting her … or maybe or maybe before we got there, I slid a movie under the seat. I rented a movie. And I slid it under the seat at Pinehurst and forgot it. And so I told her to hurry up and get her check and head straight to the movie store because it was almost late. And uh, they charge $5.00 if you don't bring them back on … Uh so we went down there and took the movie back. Uh I asked him if he had any job openings and he said no. But he let me go ahead and fill out an application and everything. And while I was doing that, she went in the grocery store and cashed her check. And uh, then when I got through, I walked on over there and helped her. I think I helped her pick out some groceries or either she was checking out or something. I don't remember. But anyway, I went over to the grocery store with her. And then we come back home and then uh I went up to Mama's and uh they told me that... uh I found out this girl I know had been shot and killed. And then I walked back down here and about ... I don't ... about 5 minutes after I got home I found out ... found out about the uh, the uh fire.

I: And that's how you found out about the fire?

S: Yeah.

I: Why were you driving Dan's car?

S: Well, he was just showing it off to me. You know about like his dog, you know. I ain't never been interested in dogs or cats. I don't have no pets. I ain't had none you know. When he takes me down there and shows me his dog and stuff ... I don't, you know ... I act interested.

I: What kind of car is it?

S: Uh, well it's uh ... I think it's a '92 Honda. Think it's a '92 Honda.

I: When did he get the car?

S: Uh, let me think. I'm really not ... I can't remember for sure when he got it.

I: Several months? A year?

S: It was ... a ... it was last ... it was last winter while I was working at the grocery store. So it had to be September or August probably of last year.

I: Do you have a valid driver's license?

S: Yeah.

I: When you were over there at Dan's house, tell me everything that you did there?

S: I don't know. We just, you know, he told me what he wanted me to do and stuff. And uh, you know, I asked him some questions about it. He said, "Well we got plenty of time." He said you'll be seeing me again before I leave and all that.

I: Start when you exited the car. What did you do?

S: Uh …

I: When you first pulled up. Pulled up in the driveway?

S: Yeah, pulled up in the driveway …

I: And then what happened?

S: And uh, and I walked down to the dog lot. I walked on down to the dog lot. And stood around there maybe, I don't know, maybe 30 seconds or a minute or two. Something like that and uh, then he told me he said the mower and stuff was up there near that door at the back of his house. Told me the mower and stuff was in there. Told me he'd get back, you know, be in touch with me and everything. Not to worry about it. That uh, that he'd be seeing me and let me know everything he wanted me to do before he left. And then right after that we left. We wasn't there but five minutes.

I: Did you go inside the house?

S: We didn't even … I didn't even go around the house.

I: What were you going to do for him while he was on vacation?

S: Well I was supposed to go in there and feed his dogs and uh, his wife's got a couple of cats. I still ain't sure I'm supposed to feed the dog twice a day. And I think the cats just one time and, you know, just keep the yard up and that's really it.

I: Where's the dog food and cat food at?

S: Uh, under the house.

I: He keeps the food under the house?

S: Well, I guess. That's where … that's where it was yesterday. He told me they'd leave everything under there where, you know, I could find everything. He told me that … well … see at the time, see that was last week, you know. He told me, you know, he'd be seeing me before, before he left or anything. He'd be seeing me again and he'd make sure that I knowed everything. I mean we … I don't know. We were just more or less killing time messing around. I was talking to him about that job.

I: Tell me about the job?

S: Well, from what he told me … what he told me was that Andy called. Uh, I think he said either Andy or Nick called him and asked him if he would open up a frame shop and build their frames. And uh, you know, I talked to him about it for about a week or something and I think Nick's wife got sick and they quit calling and you know. I don't know. We were starting to think that they were just, you know, just talking like they did before and wasn't really going to do nothing. And uh, then so the last week he had a meeting up there one morning, and uh, he told me to get back in touch with him after that meeting. To call him or something and he said that he was going to go up there and tell him that either, you know, start to make a move and show him that they were serious and were really going to do it or he just wasn't going to mess with it.

I: How did you meet Dan?

S: At work.

I: Where?

S: At Bruce Jones's.

I: At Bruce Jones's?

S: Yeah. Yeah. When I first went to work there he was a foreman and Bruce made him plant manager and then not too long after that he branched out on his own.

I: Who branched out, Dan?

S: Yes. I think Bruce leased the building, machines and stuff and just let him go in on his own because he done building, knew a ... knew frame.

I: You stated earlier that you went up to Sea Grove and you talked about a place that Bruce Jones owned, but you didn't look at it. Why didn't you look at it?

S: Well, because Bruce Jones owns it and it wouldn't do us no good to want it.

I: Why?

S: Well, because they hate each other.

I: Why do they hate each other?

S: I don't know, to be honest with you. I honestly don't know. I never really pry into it. The only thing I've ever found out, now I asked Dan one time after it just seemed like everybody was jealous, you know. Wanted Dan to fail with that shop and everything. And then when he started doing real good and people was all the time talking about him and stuff. I went in the office one day and he was setting there. Just looked like he was about to cry and it was in the middle of the day. And, uh, I didn't know what was going on or anything. I told him, I said, I told him just go on home and that I'd go ahead and take care of the shop for the rest of the day and not to worry about it. And uh, so after a few minutes, I talked him into it and he left. He told me that uh, this some ... this girl that worked up there at Bruce's shop, you know, sometimes when we was behind. Theydidn't have nothing to do you know, we might let one or two oftheir people come down there and work with us for a little while. She went up there and she told Bruce or told me and some people that he'd give her $10.00 a hour to work for him. Which you know, he might of said that joking around, but that's all you know. Just joking. There ain't no way he could of been serious about it. And then I heard from what I was told that's what the whole fight started over.

I: How often do you see Dan?

S: Uh, well ... now I see him more than I used to. I used to check with him about at least a couple times a week, you know. And uh, once in awhile my boy goes up there and buys race cars and stuff.

I: So now you see him about every day?

S: Well, no. No not every day.

I: Tell me the reason again why he picked you up here that morning?

S: Well, because ... see the day before that he had that meeting in Asheboro. And see I've been calling him or going by the store you know, regular ... if, you know, to see if they was going to open the shop up and when I might be able to go to work and everything. And he told me to call him sometime that evening. That he had a meeting up there that morning. And he told me to get back in touch with him later. And that uh, he'd tell me what happened. And when I called him he said that Nick told him that they was serious and that he was ready to put up $30,000 to get it going. And he said go ahead and find the building and get ... get it started. And Dan told me he was supposed to go on the payroll this week, Monday. And uh, so he asked me if I wanted to ride around and look at a few buildings and he had to talk to me some more. And I said all right. And he said he'd come by and pick me up and I said well I can't really look too much tomorrow because, uh Tim's got an eye doctor appointment. And I always go with him to the eye doctor, me and Anne both. And that's about it.

I: Did you know that Dan was having some financial problems?

S: No. He's always seemed to have money to me. The last … a couple weeks ago I was broke. That's the first person I thought about was Dan. I went over there and borrowed about twenty or thirty dollars.

I: How do you get along with Sally.

S: Well, I … you know. I don't really see her that much. I get along with her.

I: Why don't you really see her that much?

S: Well it's … I just don't visit his house that much when they're all there because it makes me nervous.

I: Why does it make you nervous?

S: Uh, it just, uh … I don't know. Maybe it's just that, you know, they've got a lot more than I have. I feel like I'm poor when I'm in their house. Do you know what I mean?

I: Yes, I understand.

S: That's … my wife don't like to. She's uncomfortable about going in there.

I: Does Sally like you?

S: Uh, I guess she does. She used to come up to the shop and clean and do stuff like that. Uh, well … one time we had a cookout down at the lake, you know or on somewhere. I don't know exactly where that was at. Some old place or something and uh, you know, she was down there. I've always got along with her. I just, you know, I ain't never really talked to her that much.

I: Are Dan and Sally getting along?

S: As far as I know.

I: Did you set that fire over there at Dan's house?

S: No.

I: Did Dan ask you to set the fire?

S: Naw.

I: Are you mad at Dan that you would have set the fire?

S: ... Naw. I ain't ... I ain't never had no reason to be mad at him. I mean, he's always tried to help me out, you know. Whenever he could.

I: He never asked you to set the fire?

S: ... Naw. As a matter of fact, you know, he just told me a few weeks ago that after Andy called him that ... that uh, he was going to go ahead and talk to him. And that I'd be working as soon as they got ready to do something.

I: Tim is there anything else you'd like to tell me about this situation?

S: ... Naw, not unless you need to know something.

I: Well, I can know the truth.

S: That is the truth.

I: I'd like to know everything.

S: That's all I know. I mean the only ... the only time I ever go talk to Dan is about work. I mean I have drove over there to a shop, but I mean, you know. Sometimes I feel a little bit embarrassed because I've been out of work so long and ... and everything. And, you know, there's days I've drove over to his store to ask him, you know, talk to him about something. There'd be people in there. And I might stand around for thirty minutes or something and end up leaving and not even talk to the man.

I: Where does your wife work now?

S: She ain't working.

I: She's not working?

S: Uh uh. She's wanting to ... she was turning socks. But she don't like mill work. So she said she's going to try to get her a restaurant job.

I: Everything you told me today is true and correct?

S: Yeah.

Task 3

Read through the same interview transcript presented below. When reading the transcript you will find 19 selective words or phrases that have been numbered and bolded. Identify the words or phrases in the spaces provided at the end of the transcript with the appropriate linguistic terminologies.

I: On the day of the fire, I believe it was Friday, is that right?

S: Yeah, yeah last Friday.

I: I want you to start from the time you woke up and just keep going until I tell you to stop. Tell me what you did from the time you woke up that morning.

S: All right. **Uh, well (1)** I got up and uh, took a shower and got **my (2)** clothes on and uh, I set the alarm uh, for my wife 'cause we had to take Tim to a doctor appointment at 11 o'clock in Pinehurst. **So (3)** I set the alarm where she can get up and uh and I just smoke me a couple of cigarettes and **sort of (4)** looked out the back window waiting for Dan to come up here and pick me up and then when I seen him coming up, you know I just come on out and lock the house up and everything.

I: What time was this?

S: Uh … I don't know. It was between 7 and 7:30. Uh I ain't got no clock in the living room and uh … anyway we **was gonna (5)** ride around and look at some buildings and uh you know. **Mainly (6)** I just talking to him about you know when I might be able to start work and what them people up there in Asheboro told him and stuff like that. I told that the Blackstone building was empty and uh you know asked him if he wanted to ride through the parking lot and look at it on his way up. So we rode up there, drove through the parking lot and uh you know rode around behind it and sort of looked at the building and uh left there and rode up to Sea Grove and uh … I **don't know which way we went (7)** then you know. I don't know them roads up there. **Went up to Sea Grove and he said something about (8)** … He said uh, something about a building being on down a road down there somewhere. **But (9)** it was one that Bruce Jones owned so we didn't bother looking at it. And come on left and come back and uh, he said he was going, you know, said he knowed a building over at Eagle Springs where he used to work. Anyway he used to build there or something at one time. And uh, we come on back to the … to his house and uh, you know. He was going, you know, took me back there to the dog lot. We walked down there and you know, talked about his dog and stuff like that and him going on vacation. And he told me when he went on vacation, he wanted me to come down there and feed his dog everyday. And cats and … and you know, mow and stuff like that and keep it up. And said he'd help me out with a little bit ofmoney. If I'd do that for him until I could get the work and uh … So we left there and went on up to Eagle Springs. And … he showed … showed me where to turn. Where that building was. We went down there and uh, built well. It was all growed up and everything. We didn't even get out of the car. I just circled around through there. And uh, then he told me to go up to that station up there. It was on up above where we went to the building. So I drove up there and we pulled in at the gas pumps and he gave me $10.00 for gas. And I went in and paid for the gas and come back out. And then we drove back here and he dropped me off. And uh, I went ahead and got my wife and Tim up and told her to hurry up and get ready and take him to the doctor. And we went to Pinehurst and took Tim to the doctor. And uh, and uh **after we took Tim to Pinehurst (10)**, uh, we went to Asheboro **because (11)** Anne was supposed to get her check at where she works. Well she didn't work none last week. She decided to quit and we had to go up there and get her check. Then when we got up there, they told us that they hadn't deposited the money in the bank and it'd be 2 o'clock before she could get it. So we went to the mall and got something to eat and went back and got her check. And while she was in there getting her … or maybe or maybe before we got there, I slid a movie under the seat. I rented a movie. And I slid it under the seat at Pinehurst and forgot it. And so I told her to hurry up and get her check and head straight to the movie store because it was almost late. And uh, they charge $5.00 if you don't bring them back on … Uh so we went down there and took the movie back. Uh I asked him if he had any job openings and he said no. But he let me go ahead and fill out an application and everything. And while I was doing that, she went in the grocery store and cashed her check. And uh, then when I got through, I walked on over there and helped her. I think I helped her pick out some groceries or either she was checking out or something. I **don't remember (12)**. But anyway, I went over to the grocery store with her. And then we come back home and then uh I went up to Mama's and uh they told me that ... Uh I found out this girl I know had been shot and killed. And then I walked back down here and about ... I don't ... about 5 minutes after I got home I found out ... found out about the uh, the uh fire.

I: And that's how you found out about the fire?

S: Yeah.

I: Why were you driving Dan's car?

S: Well, he was just showing it off to me. You know about like his dog, you know. I ain't never been interested in dogs or cats. I don't have no pets. I ain't had none you know. When he takes me down there and shows me his dog and stuff ... I don't, you know ... I act interested.

I: What kind of car is it?

S: Uh, well it's uh ... I think it's a '92 Honda. Think it's a '92 Honda.

I: When did he get the car?

S: Uh, let me think. I'm really not ... I can't remember for sure when he got it.

I: Several months? A year?

S: It was ... a ... it was last ... it was last winter while I was working at the grocery store. So it had to be September or August probably of last year.

I: Do you have a valid driver's license?

S: Yeah.

I: When you were over there at Dan's house, tell me everything that you did there?

S: **I don't know (13)**. **We just (14)**, you know, he told me what he wanted me to do and stuff. And uh, you know, I asked him some questions about it. He said, "Well we got plenty of time." He said you'll be seeing me again before I leave and all that.

I: Start when you exited the car? What did you do?

S: Uh …

I: When you first pulled up. Pulled up in the driveway?

S: Yeah, pulled up in the driveway …

I: And then what happened?

S: And uh, and I walked down to the dog lot. I walked on down to the dog lot. And stood around there maybe, **I don't know (15)**, maybe 30 seconds or a minute or two. Something like that and uh, then he told me he said the mower and stuff was up there near that door at the back of his house. Told me the mower and stuff was in there. Told me he'd get back, you know, be in touch with me and everything. Not to worry about it. That uh, that he'd be seeing me and let me know everything he wanted me to do before he left. And then right after that we left. We wasn't there but five minutes.

I: Did you go inside the house?

S: We didn't even … I didn't even go around the house.

I: What were you going to do for him while he was on vacation?

S: Well I was supposed to go in there and feed his dogs and uh, his wife's got a couple of cats. I still ain't sure I'm supposed to feed the dog twice a day. And I think the cats just one time and, you know, just keep the yard up and that's really it.

I: Where's the dog food and cat food at?

S: Uh, under the house.

I: He keeps the food under the house?

S: Well, I guess. That's where … that's where it was yesterday. He told me they'd leave everything under there where, you know, I could find everything. He told me that ... well ... see at the time, see that was last week, you know. He told me, you know, he'd be seeing me before, before he left or anything. He'd be seeing me again and he'd make sure that I knowed everything. I mean we ... I don't know. We were just more or less killing time messing around. I was talking to him about that job.

I: Tell me about the job?

S: **Well (16),** from what he told me ... what he told me was that Andy called. Uh, I think he said either Andy or Nick called him and asked him if he would open up a frame shop and build theirframes. And uh, you know, I talked to him about it for about a week or something and I think Nick's wife got sick and they quit calling and you know. I don't know. We were starting to think that they were just, you know, just talking like they did before and wasn't really going to do nothing. And uh, then so the last week he had a meeting up there one morning, and uh, he told me to get back in touch with him after that meeting. To call him or something and he said that he was going to go up there and tell him that either, you know, start to make a move and show him that they were serious and were really going to do it or he just wasn't going to mess with it.

I: How did you meet Dan?

S: At work.

I: Where?

S: At Bruce Jones's.

I: At Bruce Jones's?

S: Yeah. Yeah. When I first went to work there he was a foreman and Bruce made him plant manager and then not too long after that he branched out on his own.

I: Who branched out, Dan?

S: Yes. I think Bruce leased the building, machines and stuff and just let him go in on his own because he done building, knew a … knew frame.

I: You stated earlier that you went up to Sea Grove and you talked about a place that Bruce Jones owned, but you didn't look at it. Why didn't you look at it?

S: Well, because Bruce Jones owns it and it wouldn't do us no good to want it.

I: Why?

S: Well, because they hate each other.

I: Why do they hate each other?

S: I don't know, **to be honest with you (17)**. I honestly don't know. **I never really pry into it (18)**. The only thing I've ever found out, now I asked Dan one time after it just seemed like everybody was jealous, you know. Wanted Dan to fail with that shop and everything. And then when he started doing real good and people was all the time talking about him and stuff. I went in the office one day and he was setting there. Just looked like he was about to cry and it was in the middle of the day. And, uh, I didn't know what was going on or anything. I told him, I said, I told him just go on home and that I'd go ahead and take care of the shop for the rest of the day and not to worry about it. And uh, so after a few minutes, I talked him into it and he left. He told me that uh, this some … this girl that worked up there at Bruce's shop, you know, sometimes when we was behind. They didn't have nothing to do you know, we might let one or two of their people come down there and work with us for a little while. She went up there and she told Bruce or told me and some people that he'd give her $10.00 a hour to work for him. Which you know, he might of said that joking around, but that's all you know. Just joking. There ain't no way he could of been serious about it. And then I heard from what I was told that's what the whole fight started over.

I: How often do you see Dan?

S: Uh, well … now I see him more than I used to. I used to check with him about at least a couple times a week, you know. And uh, once in awhile my boy goes up there and buys race cars and stuff.

I: So now you see him about every day?

S: Well, no. No not every day.

I: Tell me the reason again why he picked you up here that morning?

S: Well, because … see the day before that he had that meeting in Asheboro. And see I've been calling him or going by the store you know, regular … if, you know, to see if they was going to open the shop up and when I might be able to go to work and everything. And he told me to call him sometime that evening. That he had a meeting up there that morning. And he told me to get back in touch with him later. And that uh, he'd tell me what happened. And when I called him he said that Nick told him that they was serious and that he was ready to put up $30,000 to get it going. And he said go ahead and find the building and get … get it started. And Dan told me he was supposed to go on the payroll this week, Monday. And uh, so he asked me if I wanted to ride around and look at a few buildings and he had to talk to me some more. And I said all right. And he said he'd come by and pick me up and I said well I can't really look too much tomorrow because, uh Tim's got an eye doctor appointment. And I always go with him to the eye doctor, me and Anne both. And that's about it.

I: Did you know that Dan was having some financial problems?

S: No. He's always seemed to have money to me. The last … a couple weeks ago I was broke. That's the first person I thought about was Dan. I went over there and borrowed about twenty or thirty dollars.

I: How do you get along with Sally.

S: Well, I … you know. I **don't really see her that much (19)**. I get along with her.

I: Why don't you really see her that much?

S: Well it's … I just don't visit his house that much when they're all there because it makes me nervous.

I: Why does it make you nervous?

S: Uh, it just, uh … I don't know. Maybe it's just that, you know, they've got a lot more than I have. I feel like I'm poor when I'm in their house. Do you know what I mean?

I: Yes, I understand.

S: That's … my wife don't like to. She's uncomfortable about going in there.

I: Does Sally like you?

S: Uh, I guess she does. She used to come up to the shop and clean and do stuff like that. Uh, well … one time we had a cookout down at the lake, you know or on somewhere. I don't know exactly where that was at. Some old place or something and uh, you know, she was down there. I've always got along with her. I just, you know, I ain't never really talked to her that much.

I: Are Dan and Sally getting along?

S: As far as I know.

I: Did you set that fire over there at Dan's house?

S: No.

I: Did Dan ask you to set the fire?

S: Naw.

I: Are you mad at Dan that you would have set the fire?

S: ... Naw. I ain't ... I ain't never had no reason to be mad at him. I mean, he's always tried to help me out, you know. Whenever he could.

I: He never asked you to set the fire?

S: ... Naw. As a matter of fact, you know, he just told me a few weeks ago that after Andy called him that ... that uh, he was going to go ahead and talk to him. And that I'd be working as soon as they got ready to do something.

I: Tim is there anything else you'd like to tell me about this situation?

S: ... Naw, not unless you need to know something.

I: Well, I can know the truth.

S: That is the truth.

I: I'd like to know everything.

S: That's all I know. I mean the only ... the only time I ever go talk to Dan is about work. I mean I have drove over there to a shop, but I mean, you know. Sometimes I feel a little bit embarrassed because I've been out of work so long and ... and everything. And, you know, there's days I've drove over to his store to ask him, you know, talk to him about something. There'd be people in there. And I might stand around for thirty minutes or something and end up leaving and not even talk to the man.

I: Where does your wife work now?

S: She ain't working.

I: She's not working?

S: Uh uh. She's wanting to … she was turning socks. But she don't like mill work. So she said she's going to try to get her a restaurant job.

I: Everything you told me today is true and correct?

S: Yeah.

Identify the linguistic terms for the corresponding words or phrases found in the transcript.

1. __________
2. __________
3. __________
4. __________
5. __________
6. __________
7. __________
8. __________
9. __________
10. __________
11. __________
12. __________
13. __________
14. __________
15. __________
16. __________
17. __________
18. __________
19. __________

Summary

The analysis of a transcript of an interview as part of an ongoing inquiry can serve as a vehicle for advancing the process. By systematically analyzing this form of discourse, more useful information may be gained from the transcript than by simply drawing a conclusion based on a general reading of the interview. The same question is repeatedly raised throughout the analysis of an interview transcript: Is the interviewee's goal to convey or to convince?

Examination

Conduct a complete analysis of the following transcript. Identify all of the significant linguistic analysis elements in the responses of the individual. Next, prepare a series of amplifying questions that correspond to those elements. Can you identify the term that is representative of the entire situation? Space has been provided at the end of the transcript.

I: Do you remember on Feb. 27th, keeping Sam for 4 days?

S: Yes.

I: On the 28th, Phyllis says she called and Sam was very upset, and said she needed to come home immediately to him, that something was wrong. Do you remember that conversation?

S: Yes, I do. I've talked with John about that. That conversation, as I recall it, Sam was sitting in my lap, talking with his Mother. I had the speaker phone on in my den, and he made the comment that he missed her, and wished she was here. To me—I took it to the point that ... that was a very nice thing for him to say. That he missed his Mother. But I don't recall any feeling that he had that he wanted her to come and get him.

I: At any time did you take the phone away from him, after he said that and start talking?

S: He was on the speaker phone 99.9 percent of the time.

I: When Sam comes and stays with you, where does he sleep in the house?

S: Well lately, and this started a year ago last Christmas when we had an over-load of people, he camped out with Grandpa in his bedroom, and he would sleep with me in my bed.

I: This started last Christmas?

S: A year ago Christmas to the best of my recollection. As I said, we had an over-load of people, even though we have four bedrooms. That was one of his favorite things since whenever he comes, he wants to camp out, as he calls it, with Grandpa.

I: Upon Sam's return home after the visit down here during the period of Feb. 27th, he alleged that you had pinched his nipples and his penis.

S: Absolutely not. As a matter of fact, when I first heard about this, this was as I recall, they had left Monday morning for home, and I expected to hear from them because they usually check in to let us know they're home, safe and sound and everything. And I hadn't heard. So Tuesday I called Phyllis, and she wasn't home. I called back maybe a half an hour later and got hold of her. And I said, "I called earlier and you weren't home." She said, "Yes, we went out to eat." I said, "that's what I figured, where'd you go?" The usual chit-chat. She said, "We went to McDonald's." And this, that, and the other. Then she said, "Here, Sam wants to talk to you." Which he always wants to talk to me. He got on the phone and the usual greetings, "You went to dinner, where'd you go? What did you have?" And this and that, and I could hear some prompting in the background. And then finally Sam says, "Grandpa, you pinched me." And I said, "I did? When was this, where did I pinch you?" And he says, "Oh, you forgot," and gave the phone back to his Mother. I says, "What's this all about?" She says, "You don't recall pinching him?" I said, "No." And then she went into a tirade about how I sexually molested her son, and that's how I heard about all of this.

I: Did you ever put your hands inside Sam's pajamas?

S: Maybe when I was putting them on him or something, tucking his shirt in.

I: Not actually after he had them on?

S: No.

I: Did you and Sam have secrets?

S: Like what?

I: Telling him not to tell anything?

S: No.

I: I want to read something to you. And if you would, after I finish reading it, just tell me what you make of it: "'What does it feel like to have a penis in your mouth?' 'Like a broom.' 'Which end?' 'Silly Mother, not the dirty end you put on the floor, the other end.' Later, he said, 'Mom, let's say the secret at the same time.' I said 'O.K. Gramps puts his penis in my mouth.' 'No, no Mom, he always does me first. He puts his mouth on my penis first, bites and licks it. And has to show me how to do it first. Then he puts his penis in my mouth. When I try to get away, he grabs my shirt, batman pajamas, and pulls me back. I'm on the floor by his bed, trying to get away. Gramps says sorry.' I recall Sam requesting batman pajamas when packing and don't forget the cape, Mom. 'Grampa looks angry when he did it. He did it once when I was a baby.'"

S: Absolutely ridiculous. I have heard, for the first time yesterday, when I was asked for a session with Dr. Brown. This is the first time that I have heard any of the accusations about anal sex, and affection for his penis, or whatever you want to refer to it as. She told me, and what she had said in front of Dr. Brown, was that "the other day, Sam came in my bedroom, and was lying on my bed. And he had an erection, and asked me to come over and suck on it." And she said, "Wait a minute, what's all this? Where did you ever hear about this?" And that Sam's reply was that, "Grampa does it to me all the time." No never.

I: When your children were young do you ever recall going in and lying on them in bed, or getting in bed with them?

S: I may have. I can recall getting them to go down for naps, and things of that nature, sure.

I: What about humping on them?

S: No. My wife asked me that, and I thought that's the most ridiculous thing I ever heard.

I: I'm going to read something else to you, and get your comment on it: "Sam is in the tub. He says, 'Grampa said if you tell your Mother the secret, pinching, oral sex, the devil will come and take your mother away. You will never see her again. She will go to jail. Mom, what is the devil? A policeman?' Dan and I both recall Sam asking earlier what a devil was: I know Sam is not making this up because Mother told me that my Father used to say this exact same thing to me and my siblings, when we were children, toddlers, to get us to make our beds, clean our rooms, etc. The devil would get you."

S: I don't recall using that kind of … I've been a God-fearing man, yes: So we've practiced our faith very religiously in our home when they were youngsters. And I'd never threaten my children, never.

I: Have you ever dressed up in a costume when Sam was around?

S: Yes, as a matter of fact, that weekend. I was dressed in a clown costume, as was my wife. We went to a Mardi-Gras party at the hotel.

I: Any other times?

S: My regalia costume.

I: What does that look like?

S: Tuxedo. We have a cape with a red lining and a sword. He referred to me as Captain Hook, the first time he saw me dressed in it.

I: Did you ever put anything in the trunk of your vehicle and take it home and cut it up when Sam was there? To be specific, I'm talking about possibly a dead animal or something like that. Where you might have ground it up in the mulcher?

S: No. Ever since I've heard about this murdered woman in the living room. And cut up her body, and took her body parts out and ran them through my shredder, and stuffed her chips in a plastic bag before we buried them in the yard. And I'm like what? What could have happened that weekend that even resembled that kind of a situation? And the only recollection I would have was that during the course of one of the days we went out and picked up pine cones. And I had him carrying a black plastic bag. And I got one of these pine cone pickers and he wanted to use that. So after a while I had him attempting to do that while I carried the bag. And then when we filled the bag, I had what I called the pine cone mountain out in the side yard. We went over there and emptied the pine cones on the pine cone mountain. I told him in time I would shred those up. And there was a little bit of a pile left from what I shredded last fall. And I remember telling him that when I put them through the shredder, that this is what happens to them. He asked me if that machine made a lot of noise, and I said, "Yes, it does." Because I know he is very conscious of loud noises. They scare him. And I said, "Yes, it makes a loud noise." I don't recall even taking him in to see it, the machine. Because if I had, I would have had to get my tractor out of the way. And pull my trailer out of the way, and everything else. Because I have that in the storage area under the house.

I: Let me read this to you: "I asked Sam to draw a picture of Gramp's penis. The size that it really is. Sam pointed out to me that the tip where the pee pee comes out. I asked him what it looked like. He said "'orange juice."' I asked him if he ever saw anything else come out of it. He said, 'yes, white milk.' I asked him where the white milk went. He said 'down your throat, and sometimes in the toilet.'"

S: That scares me. What kind of answer can I give to that? That's utterly unbelievable.

I: "Sunday, March 27th, Sam is visibly disturbed. We discuss his bad feelings. He describes being scared when he was playing in the hobby room at Gramp's house. And Grampa came into the room and jumped on top of him. We reenacted this game. Gramps knocks him down and lays on top of him. Sometimes Sam lays on top of Gramps. Sometimes Gramps smacks him in the face. Next they go into the den. Sam takes me into my bedroom. Sam pulls down the front of his pants and says, 'ere Mom put my penis in your mouth like Gramps does.' I said, 'Sam, Mothers don't do that to their sons.' Next Sam kneels on the bed with his bottom up in the air and tells me to be Gramps. I ask what am I supposed to do. He says I should put my penis in. 'Do it Mom, so I can show you how I kick him, when he does it.' I am baffled. He says to use my foot and take off my sock and pretend it is a penis. 'No Mom, your hand's got to go up here.' He puts my arms and hands slightly in front of his head. 'What does it feel like to have a penis in you, Sam.' 'Like a knife cutting me up. He also puts his finger in me sometimes.'

S: No. As I told John Smith earlier, as far as me entering Sam, that is a total physical impossibility. I have suffered from impotency since I had my prostrate surgery two years ago.

I: I've got one more thing here. This is Phyllis, when she was younger: "I can remember lying in bed at night, hearing my brother in bed crying. And my Father in there with him, talking to him. This bothered me a great deal, but I did not know what to do. I remember once at the cottage, my Father was in the bath tub with my brother during the day. I think my Father had been drinking. I was on the couch and could not sleep. But could hear my Father say, 'Haven't you got any balls in that bag?' My brother was at least 7 years old, maybe older. I wondered why my Father was feeling my brother's scrotum. My brother said something like, 'Don't Dad.' I could tell my brother was uncomfortable."

S: I have no recollection of anything like that.

I: Were you by any chance an abused child?

S: Was I?

I: Yes.

S: No.

Answers:

____

____

____

____

Chapter 9

Multiple Document Analysis Synergisms

Concept addressed in this chapter:

Combining the information gathered from the analysis of two or more documents.

Introduction

Having addressed the analysis of letters and transcripts, we can now examine the opportunities afforded within an inquiry resulting from the analysis of multiple documents. One of the most functional aspects of investigative discourse analysis occurs when the information gained from the analysis of one document is combined with that obtained from another. This analysis combination can become synergistic; taking the knowledge of the analyst to a higher level than either of the documents would have managed individually.

To illustrate the process, we will examine two documents related to the murder of JonBenét Ramsey—the ransom note and a portion of an interview transcript. In this examination, our prevailing question is, "What would the writer of the ransom note have to have known?"

Task 1

Read the wording of the ransom note which follows. Follow the process discussed in Chapter 7, identifying any linguistic components and paying attention to the full implications of the parts of speech. Answer the questions and respond to the questions that follow.

MR. RAMSEY:

Listen carefully! We are a group of individuals that represent a small foreign faction. We respect your business but not the country that it serves. At this time we have your daughter in our possession. She is safe and unharmed, and if you want her to see 1997, you must follow our instructions to the letter.

You will withdraw $118,000 from your account. $100,000 will be in $100 bills and the remaining $18,000 in $20 bills. Make sure that you bring an adequate size attaché to the bank. When you get home you will put the money in a brown paper bag. I will call you between 8 and 10 a.m. tomorrow to instruct you on delivery.

The delivery will be exhausting so I advise you to be rested. If we monitor you getting the money early, we might call you early to arrange an earlier delivery of the money and hence an earlier pickup of your daughter.

Any deviation of my instructions will result in the immediate execution of your daughter. You will also be denied her remains for proper burial. The two gentlemen watching over your daughter do not particularly like you so I advise you not to provoke them.

Speaking to anyone about your situation such as police or F.B.I, will result in your daughter being beheaded. If we catch you talking to a stray dog, she dies. If you alert bank authorities, she dies. If the money is in anyway marked or tamper with, she dies. You will be scanned for electronic devices and if any are found, she dies.

You can try to deceive us, but be warned we are familiar with law enforcement counter-measures and tactics. You stand a 99 percent chance of killing your daughter if you try to outsmart us. Follow our instructions and you stand a 100 percent chance of getting her back.

You and your family are under constant scrutiny, as well as the authorities. Don't try to grow a brain, John. You are not the only fat cat around so don't think that killing will be difficult. Don't underestimate us, John. Use that good, southern common sense of yours. It's up to you now, John! Victory. S.B.T.C.

Answer the following.

1. Identify any examples of immediacy found within the note.

____

____

____

2. Identify any examples of the pronoun *I* found within the note.

____

____

____

3. Identify any examples of introjection found within the note.

____

____

____

4. What term is used by the note writer to describe the kidnapping?

____

____

____

5. The note was found early on the morning of December 26. What word can you find that indicates the day the note was written?

____

____

____

6. The note indicated the call for delivery instructions could come as early as 8:00 in the morning of the 26th. What would the writer of the note had to have known regarding what must have transpired in order to have the money in hand by that time?

____

____

____

The second document for review involves a portion of a transcript of an interview conducted by CNN correspondent Brian Cabell with John and Patsy Ramsey, parents of JonBenét. In the interview, Cabell discusses the circumstances surrounding the death of their daughter with Mr. and Mrs. Ramsey. The interview was conducted on January 6, 1997.[1]

Task 2

Read the following transcript portion. Follow the process discussed in Chapter 8, identifying any linguistic components and paying attention to the full implications of the parts of speech. Answer the questions and respond to the questions that follow.

...

CABELL: Are you fully convinced that your daughter was kidnapped by some outsiders outside your family or circle of friends?

RAMSEY, J: Yes. I we don't you know, it's just so hard to know, but we are our family is a loving family. It's a gentle family. We have lost one child. We know how precious their lives are.

CABELL: Mrs. Ramsey you found the note. Was it a handwritten note, three pages?

RAMSEY, P: I didn't I couldn't read the whole thing I, I just gotten up. We were on our it was the day after Christmas, and we were going to go visiting, and it was quite early in the morning, and I had got dressed and was on my way to the kitchen to make some coffee, and we have a back staircase from the bedroom areas, and I always come down that staircase, and I am usually the first one down. And the note was lying across the three pages across the run of one of the stair treads, and it was kind of dimly lit. It was just very early in the morning, and I started to read it, and it was addressed to John. It said Mr. Ramsey, And it said, we have your daughter. And I you know, it just was it just wasn't registering, and I, I may have gotten

1. http://www.websleuths.org/dcforum/DCForumID70/19.html_August 9, 2011.

through another sentence. I can't we have your daughter and I don't know if I got any further than that. And I immediately ran back upstairs and pushed open her door, and she was not in her bed, and I screamed for John.

CABELL: John, you subsequently read the note. Was there anything in there that struck you in any sense?

RAMSEY, J: Well, no. I mean, I read it very fast. I was out of my mind. And it said don't call the police. You know, that type of thing. And I told Patsy, call the police immediately. And I think I ran through the house a bit.

RAMSEY, P: We went to check our son.

RAMSEY, J: Checked our son's room. Sometimes she sleeps in there. And we just were

RAMSEY, P: We were just frantic.

CABELL: How did you happen later to look in the basement?

RAMSEY, J: Well, we'd waited until after the time that the call was supposed to have been made to us, and one of the detectives asked me and my friend who was there to go through every inch of the house to see if there was anything unusual or abnormal that looked out of place.

RAMSEY, P: Look for clues I guess.

RAMSEY, J: Look for clues, asking us to do that, give us something more to do to occupy our mind, and so we started in the basement, and and we were just looking, and we one room in the basement that when I opened the door there were no windows in that room, and I turned the light on, and I that was her.

...

Answer the following:

1. List all of the linguistic components that you found in the transcript.

2. The interview revealed that Mrs. Ramsey always came down the back stairs to the kitchen. How does that information relate to the placement of the note?

3. Mrs. Ramsey states that it was "very early in the morning" when she came down the steps and found the note. How does the timing of the discovery of the note relate to the phone call coming in as early as 8 a.m.?

Summary

The analysis of multiple documents can serve to link information, thus elevating the level of what is known considerably. In these cases, the whole really is more than the sum of its parts.

Chapter 10

Sentence Deep Analysis

Concepts addressed in this chapter

The role of metaphors in the analysis process
Metaphors in a sentence
Metaphors in a narrative
Metaphors in a letter
Metaphors in a transcript

Introduction

In 1954, Theodor Seuss Geisel—Dr. Seuss—published the book ***Horton Hears a Who!*** In the story, Horton the elephant finds a speck of dust which is, in actuality, an inhabited, microscopic planet. The planet is populated by *Whos*. In Horton's effort to protect the Whos and their planet from harm, we learn that small things matter too.

The lesson holds true in investigative discourse analysis. We have progressed to the point where we can go to a deeper analysis to understand that in a sentence, small things matter too. Beyond all of the terms, concepts, and definitions we have addressed so far, there remain small—though no less important—linguistic *Whos* existing in sentences which have much to teach us.

Now, let's focus on *who and what* reside in a sentence and how they can significantly impact the productive outcome of phase three—the amplification.

An admitted fraudster made the decision to speak with agents from the Federal Bureau of Investigation and the regional Federal Prosecutor. His stated intent was to reveal the illegal activities he and his business partner had perpetrated. While testifying at his associate's trial, he stated the following regarding why he decided to turn himself in to the authorities:

> By May 20__ the funds were dwindling and I realized something had to be done. I would need to do something or everything was going to fall on me.

In the first sentence we see that there came a point in time when he arrived at the revelation that an action on his part—*something*—was needed. The term *had* indicates the option of continuing as before was no longer viable. The consideration of the range of actions that could be taken was now in play.

In the second sentence, the increase in intensity is illustrated by the term *need*. Now the individual is in an either-or situation. In his mind, the worst case scenario, if he did nothing, would be "everything falling" on him. By attending to his use of a metaphor, we can gain insight into the individual's cognitions.

Investigative discourse analysis is as much about what is *not* there as much as it is about what *is* there. He did not go to the authorities because of crisis of conscience or a realization that it is wrong to defraud others. He went because it was the least aversive of all the negative options.

Metaphors describe something in terms of what it is not. Shakespeare wrote, "Juliet is the sun!" Juliet was not really the sun, but by examining the characteristics and attributes of the sun we can gain insight into how Romeo thought of her and their relationship: she was the light of his life, everything revolved around her; without her all would be dark, cold and dead. If you want greater insight into how another person is thinking, pay attention to the metaphors they use.

For example, the words *everything falling* are ripe for fleshing (ripe and flesh are both metaphors) out. If everything could "fall" on him, then whatever constituted "everything" had to have been laid out and subsequently built up. Also it must be subject to a physical law—in this case, gravity. It had reached a point in its construction wherein it could no longer prevail against the force of gravity. The construction that constituted "everything" was no longer sustainable. Additionally since it would eventually "fall on" him, he had to be under all that made up "everything."

So, how does this deeper, metaphor-focused analysis assist in the conduct of the interview in phase three? The goal in phase three is to achieve alterity—the ability to go into another person's world and understand how that world operates. We use that understanding to assist in our efforts to gain compliance, cooperation, admissions, and confessions. We want to use those same metaphors in conducting our interviews. For example:

Initial question:

> Jim, you said everything would fall on you, tell me about that?

Subsequent questions on the same topic:

> Jim, what would have caused everything to fall? Jim, why would it have fallen on you?

Now we will examine another quote from this same individual. In his testimony, he revealed his rationalization for his continued diversion of assets and deception even after having gone to the federal authorities. He testified:

> At some point in the future I hoped to sell the items to get back on my feet.

"At some point in the future ..." Here he references a location, a point. He is a time traveler on his way to the future. Eventually in the future he will reach a specific destination and upon doing so there is an action (sell what he had stolen from others) he will undertake.

" ... to get back on my feet." During this passage of time, he will be off of his feet. People who are off of their feet are limited, restricted, or destitute. He will, sometime in the future, convert what belongs to others to himself, thus getting back on his feet. That which he stole, knocking others off of their feet, will be used to help him gain his footing at the appropriate time in the future. Now we understand that his fraudulent mindset has not changed. Even after going to the authorities and testifying against his associate, he continued to "hope" to use that which belonged to others to help him have a better life.

Task 1

Write out two open, non-specific questions you would ask based on the metaphors in the second quote above.

____

____

____

Task 2

Examine the following quote. Extrapolate the information found in the quote and write the questions you determine necessary to amplify what the interviewee has asserted.

> I got short on funds, because here I was living two lives. And the opportunity came … presented itself for me to commit the fraud that I committed.

____

____

____

____

____

Task 3

Read the following narrative. Locate and list the metaphors found within the narrative.

Extrapolate the implications of each metaphor. Develop the amplifying questions with the appropriate terminologies to address each metaphor. Space has been provided at the end of the narrative for your response.

> My name is Jane Doe. I was hired by Bank on December 6, ____. After the completion of training I was sent to Banking Center on Jan. 22, ____ as a part time teller. I was employed by the bank a little less than one month when I saw something that I was not supposed to see. I saw Ann Jones taking money from a deposit bag one morning. When

she saw that I saw what she was doing,she said, "please don't tell, I'll give you half. How much do you want?" My answer to her was, "what you do is none of my business." That ended for the time being. About a week or two later I was talking about my hair. I told everyone how I needed a hair-do. Ann offered me some money if I would help her out. I asked what kind of help she was talking about and she gave me a piece of a paper about one hour later that said use a debit memo, record information as is and we'll split. I fell into temptation and did the transaction. I asked her what to do with the money and she said hold it. I began to feel very uneasy so I took the money to her and asked for change (quarters) with about forty dollars. She said being secretive and sneaky would get me caught. She gave me my share of the money near the supply closet. She gave a hundred and fifty dollars. She said thanks and that I could make more than that. About a week later, she did the same thing (another debit memo). This one was bigger and I was more nervous than before but I did it. She gave me the information. This one was one thousand dollars but this person was already one of my customers early. I gave her the money the same way I did before. She did not give me my share until after hours but it was only three hundred dollars. I asked how come she got so much more and she replied, "three-way split." I told her that I still should have received more than three hundred but she said that she would take care of me. I asked about the third person and she asked if I really wanted to know or be left out of it. I dropped it thinking that if it all came back it wouldn't come back to me but it did. There were two more for the same amount but it was always a three-way split. Then on March 12, ____, I did a debit memo from (the consumer bankers) in the amount of $2000 from John Jones, M.D. In order to cash this I needed an override from a supervisor. Mel completed the override and I have the customer copy and the money to the consumer banker, either Minnie or Daisy. I do not want to hurt anyone else but I honestly can't remember which one. Not to say Daisy would but I don't believe Minnie would hurt me intentionally. This is my confession, I am sorry for hurting the innocent customers and I gave back the money I received because I was afraid to spend it anyway. Sorry for everything.

Jane Doe

Task 4

Locate the metaphors in the following letter. Write each metaphor and extrapolate its meaning and insight into the individual's world. It will enhance the learning process to write it. Write an open, non-specific question for each metaphor. Space has been provided at the end of the letter for your response.

> Dear Mary,
>
> People will say that by my actions I am a guilty man. That I was a monster. That I was insane. But you know I would never have touched my children in an immoral way and my children know the truth. This I swear on my soul. My life has never been easy and I know that my paths are my own choosing. You and the kids brought me the only happiness I have ever known. I love you all dearly but I cannot stand this. To the people who hated me so, you can say they won. I just can't face the future not knowing if I can have my kids and you. I was not a perfect husband and father but I was no child molester either. Please find out who was. Tell Mom, Scott and Jane that I love them. But I have been broken. Under no circumstances let me be buried in the family cemetery. Cremate me if you have to. I don't care. My heart's too broke to care. I just can't deal with the shame of these accusations anymore. And you can tell Anne and Patty and Donna and the rest of your family that if there is a way to come back I will find it. I feel such hate for them it consumes me. I'm sorry. Please forgive me and as the God I will soon see is my witness I have never violated my children.

____

____

____

____

____

____

____

____

____

____

____

____

Task 5

The following is an interview with O.J. Simpson. Identify any metaphors used by the interviewee and the interviewers. List the metaphors under the name of each speaker. What can you extrapolate from the interviewee's metaphors? What adjustments in terminology would you make to allow you to connect to the cognitions of the interviewee? Space has been provided at the end of the transcript for your response.

Vannatter: ... my partner, Detective Lange, and we're in an interview room in Parker Center. The date is June 13th, 1994, and the time is 13:35 hours. And we're here with O.J. Simpson. Is that Orenthal James Simpson?

Simpson: Orenthal James Simpson

Vannatter: And what is your birthdate, Mr. Simpson?

Simpson: July 9th, 1947.

Vannatter: OK. Prior to us talking to you, as we agreed with your attorney, I'm going to give you your constitutional rights. And I would like you to listen carefully. If you don't understand anything, tell me, OK?

Simpson: All right

Vannatter: OK. Mr. Simpson, you have the right to remain silent. If you give up the right to remain silent, anything you say can and will be used against you in a court of law. You have the right to speak to an attorney and to have an attorney present during the questioning. If you so desire and cannot afford one, an attorney will be appointed for you without charge before questioning. Do you understand your rights?

Simpson: Yes, I do.

Vannatter: Are there any questions about that?

Simpson: (unintelligible)

Vannatter: OK, you've got to speak up louder than that …

Simpson: OK, no.

Vannatter: OK, do you wish to give up your right to remain silent and talk to us?

Simpson: Ah, yes.

Vannatter: OK, and you give up your right to have an attorney present while we talk?

Simpson: Mmm hmm. Yes.

Vannatter: OK. All right, what we're gonna do is, we want to…. We're investigating, obviously, the death of your ex-wife and another man.

Lange: Someone told us that.

Vannatter: Yeah, and we're going to need to talk to you about that. Are you divorced from her now?

Simpson: Yes.

Vannatter: How long have you been divorced?

Simpson: Officially? Probably close to two years, but we've been apart for a little over two years.

Vannatter: Have you?

Simpson: Yeah.

Vannatter: What was your relationship with her? What was the …

Simpson: Well, we tried to get back together, and it just didn't work. It wasn't working, and so we were going our separate ways.

Vannatter: Recently you tried to get back together?

Simpson: We tried to get back together for about a year, you know, where we started dating each other and seeing each other. She came back and wanted us to get back together, and …

Vannatter: Within the last year, you're talking about?

Simpson: She came back about a year and four months ago about us trying to get back together, and we gave it a shot. We gave it a shot the better part of a year. And I think we both knew it wasn't working, and probably three weeks ago or so, we said it just wasn't working, and we went our separate ways.

Vannatter: OK, the two children are yours?

Simpson: Yes.

Lange: She have custody?

Simpson: We have joint custody.

Lange: Through the courts?

Simpson: We went through the courts and everything. Everything is done. We have no problems with the kids, we do everything together, you know, with the kids.

Vannatter: How was your separation? What that a … ?

Simpson: The first separation?

Vannatter: Yeah, was there problems with that?

Simpson: For me, it was big problems. I loved her, I didn't want us to separate.

Vannatter: Uh huh. I understand she had made a couple of crime … crime reports or something?

Simpson: Ah, we have a big fight about six years ago on New Year's, you know, she made a report. I didn't make a report. And then we had an altercation about a year ago maybe. It wasn't a physical argument. I kicked her door or something.

Vannatter: And she made a police report on those two occasions?

Simpson: Mmm hmm. And I stayed right there until the police came, talked to them.

Lange: Were you arrested at one time for something?

Simpson: No. I mean, five years ago we had a big fight, six years ago. I don't know. I know I ended up doing community service.

Vannatter: So you weren't arrested?

Simpson: No, I was never really arrested.

Lange: They never booked you or …

Simpson: No.

Vannatter: Can I ask you, when's the last time you've slept?

Simpson: I got a couple of hours sleep last night. I mean, you know, I slept a little on the plane, not much, and when I got to the hotel I was asleep a few hours when the phone call came.

Lange: Did Nicole have a housemaid that lived there?

Simpson: I believe so, yes.

Lange: Do you know her name at all?

Simpson: Evia, Elvia, something like that.

Vannatter: We didn't see her there. Did she have the day off perhaps?

Simpson: I don't know. I don't know what schedule she's on.

Lange: Phil, what do you think? We can maybe just recount last night …

Vannatter: Yeah. When was the last time you saw Nicole?

Simpson: We were leaving a dance recital. She took off and I was talking to her parents.

Vannatter: Where was the dance recital?

Simpson: Paul Revere High School.

Vannatter: And was that for one of your children?

Simpson: Yeah, for my daughter Sydney.

Vannatter: And what time was that yesterday?

Simpson: It ended about 6:30, quarter to seven, something like that, you know, in the ballpark, right in that area. And they took off.

Vannatter: They?

Simpson: Her and her family—her mother and father, sisters, my kids, you know.

Vannatter: And then you went your own separate way?

Simpson: Yeah, actually she left, and then they came back and her mother got in a car with her, and the kids all piled into her sister's car, and they …

Vannatter: Was Nicole driving?

Simpson: Yeah.

Vannatter: What kind of car was she driving?

Simpson: Her black car, a Cherokee, a Jeep Cherokee.

Vannatter: What were you driving?

Simpson: My Rolls Royce, my Bentley.

Vannatter: Do you own that Ford Bronco that sits outside?

Simpson: Hertz owns it, and Hertz lets me use it.

Vannatter: So that's your vehicle, the one that was parked there on the street?

Simpson: Mmm hmm.

Vannatter: And it's actually owned by Hertz?

Simpson: Hertz, yeah.

Vannatter: Who's the primary driver on that? You?

Simpson: I drive it, the housekeeper drives it, you know, it's kind of a …

Vannatter: All-purpose type vehicle?

Simpson: All-purpose, yeah. It's the only one that my insurance will allow me to let anyone else drive.

Vannatter: OK

Lange: When you drive it, where do you park it at home? Where it is now, it was in the street or something?

Simpson: I always park it on the street.

Lange: You never take it in the …

Simpson: Oh, rarely. I mean, I'll bring it in—and switch the stuff, you know, and stuff like that. I did that yesterday, you know.

Lange: When did you last drive it?

Simpson: Yesterday.

Vannatter: What time yesterday?

Simpson: In the morning, in the afternoon.

Vannatter: OK, you left her, you're saying, about 6:30 or 7, or she left the recital?

Simpson: Yeah.

Vannatter: And you spoke with her parents?

Simpson: Yeah, we were just sitting there talking.

Vannatter: OK, what time did you leave the recital?

Simpson: Right about that time. We were all leaving. We were all leaving then. Her mother said something about me joining them for dinner, and I said no thanks.

Vannatter: Where did you go from there, O.J.?

Simpson: Ah, home, home for a while, got my car for a while, tried to find my girlfriend for a while, came back to the house.

Vannatter: Who was home when you got home?

Simpson: Kato.

Vannatter: Kato? Anybody else? Was your daughter there, Arnelle?

Simpson: No.

Vannatter: Isn't that her name, Arnelle?

Simpson: Arnelle, yeah.

Vannatter: So what time do you think you got back home, actually physically got home?

Simpson: Seven-something.

Vannatter: Seven-something? And then you left, and ...

Simpson: Yeah, I'm trying to think, did I leave? You know, I'm always … I had to run and get my daughter some flowers. I was actually doing the recital, so I rushed and got her some flowers, and I came home, and then I called Paula as I was going to her house, and Paula wasn't home.

Vannatter: Paula is your girlfriend?

Simpson: Girlfriend, yeah.

Vannatter: Paula who?

Simpson: Barbieri.

Vannatter: Could you spell that for me?

Simpson: B-A-R-B-I-E-R-I.

Vannatter: Do you know an address on her?

Simpson: No, she lives on Wilshire, but I think she's out of town.

Vannatter: You got a phone number?

Simpson: Yeah (number deleted by STAR).

Vannatter: So you didn't see her last night?

Simpson: No, we'd been to a big affair the night before, and then I came back home. I was basically at home. I mean, any time I was … whatever time it took me to get to the recital and back, to get to the flower shop and back, I mean, that's the time I was out of the house.

Vannatter: Were you scheduled to play golf this morning, some place?

Simpson: In Chicago.

Vannatter: What kind of tournament was it?

Simpson: Ah, it was Hertz, with special clients.

Vannatter: Oh, OK. What time did you leave last night, leave the house?

Simpson: To go to the airport?

Vannatter: Mmm hmm.

Simpson: About ... the limo was supposed to be there at 10:45. Normally, they get there a little earlier. I was rushing around — somewhere between there and 11.

Vannatter: So approximately 10:45 to 11.

Simpson: Eleven o'clock, yea, somewhere in that area.

Vannatter: And you went by limo?

Simpson: Yeah.

Vannatter: Who's the limo service?

Simpson: Ah, you have to ask my office.

Lange: Did you converse with the driver at all? Did you talk to him?

Simpson: No, he was a new driver. Normally, I have a regular driver I drive with and converse. No, just about rushing to the airport, about how I live my life on airplanes, and hotels, that type of thing.

Lange: What time did the plane leave?

Simpson: Ah, 11:45 the flight took off.

Vannatter: What airline was it?

Simpson: American.

Vannatter: American? And it was 11:45 to Chicago?

Simpson: Chicago.

Lange: So yesterday you did drive the white Bronco?

Simpson: Mmm hmm.

Lange: And where did you park it when you brought it home?

Simpson: Ah, the first time probably by the mailbox. I'm trying to think, or did I bring it in the driveway? Normally, I will park it by the mailbox, sometimes ...

Lange: On Ashford, or Ashland?

Simpson: On Ashford, yeah.

Lange: Where did you park yesterday for the last time, do you remember?

Simpson: Right where it is.

Lange: Where it is now?

Simpson: Yeah.

Lange: Where, on … ?

Simpson: Right on the street there.

Lange: On Ashford?

Simpson: No, on Rockingham.

Lange: You parked it there?

Simpson: Yes.

Lange: About what time was that?

Simpson: Eight-something, seven … eight, nine o'clock, I don't know, right in that area.

Lange: Did you take it to the recital?

Simpson: No.

Lange: What time was the recital?

Simpson: Over at about 6:30. Like I said, I came home, I got my car, I was going to see my girlfriend. I was calling her and she wasn't around.

Lange: So you drove the … you came home in the Rolls, and then you got in the Bronco …

Simpson: In the Bronco, 'cause my phone was in the Bronco. And because it's a Bronco. It's a Bronco, it's what I drive, you know. I'd rather drive it than any other car. And, you know, as I was going over there, I called her a couple of times and she wasn't there, and I left a message, and then I checked my messages, and there were no new messages. She wasn't there, and she may have to leave town. Then I came back and ended up sitting with Kato.

Lange: OK, what time was this again that you parked the Bronco?

Simpson: Eight-something, maybe. He hadn't done a Jacuzzi, we had ... went and got a burger, and I'd come home and kind of leisurely got ready to go. I mean, we'd done a few things ...

Lange: You weren't in a hurry when you came back with the Bronco.

Simpson: No

Lange: The reason I asked you, the cars were parked kind of at a funny angle, stuck out in the street.

Simpson: Well, it's parked because ... I don't know if it's a funny angle or what. It's parked because when I was hustling at the end of the day to get all my stuff, and I was getting my phone and everything off it, when I just pulled it out of the gate there, it's like it's a tight turn.

Lange: So you had it inside the compound, then?

Simpson: Yeah.

Lange: Oh, OK.

Simpson: I brought it inside the compound to get my stuff out of it, and then I put it out, and I'd run back inside the gate before the gate closes.

Vannatter: What's your office phone number?

Simpson: (number deleted by STAR)

Vannatter: And is that area code 310?

Simpson: Yes.

Vannatter: How did you get the injury on your hand?

Simpson: I don't know. The first time, when I was in Chicago and all, but at the house I was just running around.

Vannatter: How did you do it in Chicago?

Simpson: I broke a glass. One of you guys had just called me, and I was in the bathroom, and I just kind of went bonkers for a little bit.

Lange: Is that how you cut it?

Simpson: Mmm, it was cut before, but I think I just opened it again, I'm not sure.

Lange: Do you recall bleeding at all in your truck, in the Bronco?

Simpson: I recall bleeding at my house and then I went to the Bronco. The last thing I did before I left, when I was rushing, was went and got my phone out of the Bronco.

Lange: Mmm hmm. Where's the phone now?

Simpson: In my bag.

Lange: You have it ... ?

Simpson: In that black bag.

Lange: You brought a bag with you here?

Simpson: Yeah, it's ...

Lange: So do you recall bleeding at all?

Simpson: Yeah, I mean, I knew I was bleeding, but it was no big deal. I bleed all the time. I play golf and stuff, so there's always something, nicks and stuff here and there.

Lange: So did you do anything? When did you put the Band-Aid on it?

Simpson: Actually, I asked the girl this morning for it.

Lange: And she got it?

Simpson: Yeah, 'cause last night with Kato, when I was leaving, he was saying something to me, and I was rushing to get my phone, and I put a little thing on it, and it stopped.

Vannatter: Do you have the keys to that Bronco?

Simpson: Yeah.

Vannatter: OK. We've impounded the Bronco. I don't know if you know that or not.

Simpson: No.

Vannatter: … take a look at it. Other than you, who's the last person to drive it.

Simpson: Probably Gigi. When I'm out of town, I don't know who drives the car, maybe my daughter, maybe Kato.

Vannatter: The keys are available?

Simpson: I leave the keys there, you know, when Gigi's there because sometimes she needs it, or Gigi was off and wasn't coming back until today, and I was coming back tonight.

Vannatter: So you don't mind if Gigi uses it, or …

Simpson: This is the only one I can let her use. When she doesn't have her car, 'cause sometimes her husband takes her car, I let her use the car.

Lange: When was the last time you were at Nicole's house?

Simpson: I don't go in, I won't go in her house. I haven't been in her house in a week, maybe five days. I go to her house a lot. I mean, I'm always dropping the kids off, picking the kids up, fooling around with the dog, you know.

Vannatter: How does that usually work? Do you drop them at the porch, or do you go in with them?

Simpson: No, I don't go in the house.

Vannatter: Is there a kind of gate out front?

Simpson: Yeah.

Vannatter: But you never go inside the house?

Simpson: Up until about five days, six days ago, I haven't been in the house. Once I started seeing Paula again, I kind of avoid Nicole.

Vannatter: Is Nicole seeing anybody else that you …

Simpson: I have no idea. I really have absolutely no idea. I don't ask her. I don't know. Her and her girlfriends, they go out, you know, they've got some things going on right now with her girlfriends, so I'm assuming something's happening because one of the girlfriends is having a big problem with her husband because she's always saying she's with Nicole until three or four in the morning. She's not. You know, Nicole tells me she leaves her at 1:30 or 2 or 2:30, and the girl doesn't get home until 5, and she only lives a few blocks away.

Vannatter: Something's going on, huh?

Lange: Do you know where they went, the family, for dinner last night?

Simpson: No. Well, no, I didn't ask.

Lange: I just thought maybe there's a regular place that they go.

Simpson: No. If I was with them, we'd go to Toscano. I mean, not Toscano, Poponi's.

Vannatter: You haven't had any problems with her lately, have you, O.J.?

Simpson: I always have problems with her, you know? Our relationship has been a problem relationship. Probably lately for me, and I say this only because I said it to Ron yesterday at the — Ron Fishman, whose wife is Cora — at the dance recital, when he came up to me and went, "Oooh, boy, what's going on?" and everybody was beefing with everybody. And I said, "Well, I'm just glad I'm out of the mix." You know, because I was like dealing with him and his problems with his wife and Nicole and evidently some new problems that a guy named Christian was having with his girl, and he was staying at Nicole's house, and something was going on, but I don't think it's pertinent to this.

Vannatter: Did Nicole have words with you last night?

Simpson: Pardon me?

Vannatter: Did Nicole have words with you last night?

Simpson: No, not at all.

Vannatter: Did you talk to her last night?

Simpson: To ask to speak to my daughter, to congratulate my daughter, and everything.

Vannatter: But you didn't have a conversation with her?

Simpson: No, no.

Vannatter: What were you wearing last night, O.J.?

Simpson: What did I wear on the golf course yesterday? Some of these kind of pants, some of these kind of pants—I mean I changed different for whatever it was. I just had on some ...

Vannatter: Just these black pants.

Simpson: Just these ... They're called Bugle Boy.

Vannatter: These aren't the pants?

Simpson: No.

Vannatter: Where are the pants that you wore?

Simpson: They're hanging in my closet.

Vannatter: These are washable, right? You just throw them in the laundry?

Simpson: Yeah, I got 100 pair. They give them to me free, Bugle Boys, so I've got a bunch of them.

Vannatter: Do you recall coming home and hanging them up, or ... ?

Simpson: I always hang up my clothes. I mean, it's rare that I don't hang up my clothes unless I'm laying them in my bathroom for her to do something with them, but those are the only things I don't hang up. But when you play golf, you don't necessarily dirty pants.

Lange: What kind of shoes were you wearing?

Simpson: Tennis shoes.

Lange: Tennis shoes? Do you know what kind?

Simpson: Probably Reebok, that's all I wear.

Lange: Are they at home, too?

Simpson: Yeah

Lange: Was this supposed to be a short trip to Chicago, so you didn't take a whole lot?

Simpson: Yeah, I was coming back today.

Lange: Just overnight?

Simpson: Yeah.

Vannatter: That's a hectic schedule, drive back here to play golf and come back.

Simpson: Yeah, but I do it all the time.

Vannatter: Do you?

Simpson: Yeah. That's what I was complaining with the driver about, you know, about my whole life is on and off airplanes.

Vannatter: O.J., we've got sort of a problem.

Simpson: Mmm hmm.

Vannatter: We've got some blood on and in your car, we've got some blood at your house, and sort of a problem.

Simpson: Well, take my blood test.

Lange: Well, we'd like to do that. We've got, of course, the cut on your finger that you aren't real clear on. Do you recall having that cut on your finger the last time you were at Nicole's house?

Simpson: A week ago?

Lange: Yeah.

Simpson: No. It was last night.

Lange: OK, so last night you cut it.

Vannatter: Somewhere after the recital?

Simpson: Somewhere when I was rushing to get out of my house.

Vannatter: OK, after the recital.

Simpson: Yeah.

Vannatter: What do you think happened? Do you have any idea?

Simpson: I have no idea, man. You guys haven't told me anything. I have no idea. When you said to my daughter, who said something to me today, that somebody else might have been involved, I have absolutely no idea what happened. I don't know how, why or what. But you guys haven't told me anything. Every time I ask you guys, you say you're going to tell me in a bit.

Vannatter: Well, we don't know a lot of answers to these questions yet ourselves, O.J., OK?

Simpson: I've got a bunch of guns, guns all over the place. You can take them, they're all there. I mean, you can see them. I keep them in my car for an incident that happened a month ago that my in-laws, my wife and everybody knows about that.

Vannatter: What was that?

Simpson: Going down to ... and cops down there know about it because I've told two marshals about it. At a mall, I was going down for a christening, and I had just left—and it was like 3:30 in the morning, and I'm in a lane, and also the car in front of me is going real slow, and I'm slowing down 'cause I figure he sees a cop, 'cause we were all going pretty fast. And I'm going to change lanes, but there's a car next to me, and I can't change lanes. Then that goes for a while, and I'm going to slow down and go around him but the car butts up to me, and I'm like caught between three cars. They were Oriental guys, and they were not letting me go anywhere. And finally I went on the shoulder, and I sped up, and then I held my phone up so they could see the light part of it, you know, 'cause I have tinted windows, and they kind of scattered, and I chased one of them for a while to make him think I was chasing him before I took off.

Lange: Were you in the Bronco?

Simpson: No.

Lange: What were you driving?

Simpson: My Bentley. It has tinted windows and all, so I figured they thought they had a nice little touch …

Lange: Did you think they were trying to rip you off?

Simpson: Definitely, they were. And then the next thing, you know, Nicole and I went home. At four in the morning I got there to Laguna, and when we woke up, I told her about it, and told her parents about it, told everybody about it, you know? And when I saw two marshals at a mall, I walked up and told them about it.

Vannatter: What did they do, make a report on it?

Simpson: They didn't know nothing. I mean, they'll remember me and remember I told them.

Vannatter: Did Nicole mention that she'd been getting any threats lately to you? Anything she was concerned about or the kids' safety?

Simpson: To her?

Vannatter: Yes.

Simpson: From?

Vannatter: From anybody.

Simpson: No, not at all.

Vannatter: Was she very security conscious? Did she keep that house locked up?

Simpson: Very.

Vannatter: The intercom didn't work apparently, right?

Simpson: I thought it worked.

Vannatter: Oh, OK. Does the electronic buzzer work?

Simpson: The electronic buzzer works to let people in.

Vannatter: Do you ever park in the rear when you go over there?

Simpson: Most of the time.

Vannatter: You do park in the rear.

Simpson: Most times when I'm taking the kids there, I come right into the driveway, blow the horn, and she, or a lot of times the housekeeper, either the housekeeper opens or they'll keep a garage door open up on the top of the thing, you know, but that's when I'm dropping the kids off, and I'm not going in — times I go to the front because the kids have to hit the buzzer and stuff.

Vannatter: Did you say before that up until about three weeks ago you guys were going out again and trying to …

Simpson: No, we'd been going out for about a year, and then the last six months we've had … it ain't been working, so we tried various things to see if we can make it work. We started trying to date, and that wasn't working, and so, you know, we just said the hell with it, you know.

Vannatter: And that was about three weeks ago?

Simpson: Yeah, about three weeks ago.

Vannatter: So you were seeing her up to that point?

Simpson: It's, it's … seeing her, yeah, I mean, yeah. It was a done deal. It just wasn't happening. I mean, I was gone. I was in San Juan doing a film, and I don't think we had sex since I've been back from San Juan, and that was like two months ago. So it's been like … for the kids we tried to do things together, you know, we didn't really date each other. Then we decided let's try to date each other. We went out one night, and it just didn't work.

Vannatter: When you say it didn't work, what do you mean?

Simpson: Ah, the night we went out it was fun. Then the next night we went out it was actually when I was down in Laguna, and she didn't want to go out. And I said, "Well, let's go out 'cause I came all the way down here to go out," and we kind of had a beef. And it just didn't work after that, you know? We were only trying to date to see if we could bring some romance back into our relationship. We just said, let's treat each other like boyfriend and girlfriend instead of, you know, like 17-year-old married people. I mean, 17 years together, whatever that is.

Vannatter: How long were you together?

Simpson: Seventeen years.

Vannatter: Seventeen years. Did you ever hit her, O.J.?

Simpson: Ah, one night we had a fight. We had a fight, and she hit me. And they never took my statement, they never wanted to hear my side, and they never wanted to hear the housekeeper's side. Nicole was drunk. She did her thing, she started tearing up my house, you know? I didn't punch her or anything, but I …

Vannatter: … slapped her a couple of times.

Simpson: No, no, I wrestled her, is what I did. I didn't slap her at all. I mean, Nicole's a strong girl. She's a … one of the most conditioned women. Since that period of time, she's hit me a few times, but I've never touched her after that, and I'm telling you, it's five-six years ago.

Vannatter: What is her birth date?

Simpson: May 19th.

Vannatter: Did you get together with her on her birthday?

Simpson: Yeah, her and I and the kids, I believe.

Vannatter: Did you give her a gift?

Simpson: I gave her a gift.

Vannatter: What did you give her?

Simpson: I gave her either a bracelet or the earrings.

Vannatter: Did she keep them or …

Simpson: Oh, no, when we split she gave me both the earrings and the bracelet back. I bought her a very nice bracelet—I don't know if it was Mother's Day or her birthday—and I bought her the earrings for the other thing, and when we split—and it's a credit to her—she felt that it wasn't right that she had it, and I said good because I want them back.

Vannatter: Was that the very day of her birthday, May 19, or was it a few days later?

Simpson: What do you mean?

Vannatter: You gave it to her on the 19th of May, her birthday, right, this bracelet?

Simpson: I may have given her the earrings. No, the bracelet, May 19th. When was Mother's Day?

Vannatter: Mother's Day was around that …

Simpson: No, it was probably her birthday, yes.

Vannatter: And did she return it the same day?

Simpson: Oh, no, she … I'm in a funny place here on this, all right? She returned it—both of them—three weeks ago or so, because when I say I'm in a funny place on this it was because I gave it to my girlfriend and told her it was for her, and that was three weeks ago. I told her I bought it for her. You know? What am I going to do with it?

Lange: Did Mr. Weitzman, your attorney, talk to you anything about this polygraph we brought up before? What are your thoughts on that?

Simpson: Should I talk about my thoughts on that? I'm sure eventually I'll do it, but it's like I've got some weird thoughts now. I've had weird thoughts ... you know when you've been with a person for 17 years, you think everything. I've got to understand what this thing is. If it's true blue, I don't mind doing it.

Lange: Well, you're not compelled at all to take this thing, number one, and number two — I don't know if Mr. Weitzman explained it to you — this goes to the exclusion of someone as much as the inclusion so we can eliminate people. And just to get things straight.

Simpson: But does it work for elimination?

Lange: Oh, yes. We use it for elimination more than anything.

Simpson: Well, I'll talk to him about it.

Lange: Understand, the reason we're talking to you is because you're the ex-husband.

Simpson: I know, I'm the number one target, and now you tell me I've got blood all over the place.

Lange: Well, there's blood at your house in the driveway, and we've got a search warrant, and we're going to go get the blood. We found some in your house. Is that your blood that's there?

Simpson: If it's dripped, it's what I dripped running around trying to leave.

Lange: Last night?

Simpson: Yeah, and I wasn't aware that it was ... I was aware that I ... You know, I was trying to get out of the house. I didn't even pay any attention to it, I saw it when I was in the kitchen, and I grabbed a napkin or something, and that was it. I didn't think about it after that.

Vannatter: That was last night after you got home from the recital, when you were rushing?

Simpson: That was last night when I was ... I don't know what I was ... I was in the car getting my junk out of the car. I was in the house throwing hangers and stuff in my suitcase. I was doing my little crazy what I do … I mean, I do it everywhere. Anybody who has ever picked me up says that O.J.'s a whirlwind, he's running, he's grabbing things, and that's what I was doing.

Vannatter: Well, I'm going to step out and I'm going to get a photographer to come down and photograph your hand there. And then here pretty soon we're going to take you downstairs and get some blood from you. OK? I'll be right back.

Lange: So it was about five days ago you last saw Nicole? Was it at the house?

Simpson: OK, the last time I saw Nicole, physically saw Nicole … I saw her obviously last night. The time before, I'm trying to think … I went to Washington, DC, so I didn't see her, so I'm trying to think … I haven't seen her since I went to Washington – what's the date today?

Lange: Today's Monday, the 13th of June.

Simpson: OK, I went to Washington on maybe Wednesday. Thursday I think I was in … Thursday I was in Connecticut, then Long Island Thursday afternoon and all of Friday. I got home Friday night, Friday afternoon. I played, you know … Paula picked me up at the airport. I played golf Saturday, and when I came home I think my son was there. So I did something with my son. I don't think I saw Nicole at all then. And then I went to a big affair with Paula Saturday night, and I got up and played golf Sunday which pissed Paula off, and I saw Nicole at … It was about a week before, I saw her at the …

Lange: OK, the last time you saw Nicole, was that at her house?

Simpson: I don't remember. I wasn't in her house, so it couldn't have been at her house, so it was, you know, I don't physically remember the last time I saw her. I may have seen her even jogging one day.

Lange: Let me get this straight. You've never physically been inside the house?

Simpson: Not in the last week.

Lange: Ever. I mean, how long has she lived there? About six months?

Simpson: Oh, Christ, I've slept all at the house many, many, many times, you know? I've done everything at the house, you know? I'm just saying , … You're talking in the last week or so.

Lange: Well, whatever. Six months she's lived there?

Simpson: I don't know. Roughly. I was at her house maybe two weeks ago, 10 days ago. One night her and I had a long talk, you know, about how can we make it better for the kids, and I told her we'd do things better. And, OK, I can almost say when that was. That was when I … I don't know, it was about 10 days ago. And then we … The next day I had her have her dog do a flea bath or something with me. Oh, I'll tell you, I did see her one day. One day I went … I don't know if this was the early part of last week, I went 'cause my son had to go and get something, and he ran in, and she came to the gate, and the dog ran out, and her friend Faye and I went looking for the dog. That may have been a week ago, I don't know.

Lange: (To Vannatter) Got a photographer coming?

Vannatter: No, we're going to take him up there.

Lange: We're ready to terminate this at 14:07

Summary

It has often been said that the eyes are the windows to the soul. If that is the case, and we believe it to be true, then metaphors are the portals into the world-conceptualizations of the speaker. Whether found on paper, a computer screen, or spoken in the conduct an interview, metaphors allow us to enter into another world and determine its operation, circumstances, and rationalizations. At the end of it all, that is exactly the primary function of investigative discourse analysis.